The Inca Empire

An Enthralling Overview of the Incas, Their Civilization in Ancient Peru, and the Spanish Conquest

Free limited time bonus

Stop for a moment. We have a free bonus set up for you. The problem is this: we forget 90% of everything that we read after 7 days. Crazy fact, right? Here's the solution: we've created a printable, 1-page pdf summary for this book that you're reading now. All you have to do to get your free pdf summary is to go to the following website:

https://livetolearn.lpages.co/enthrallinghistory/

Once you do, it will be intuitive. Enjoy, and thank you!

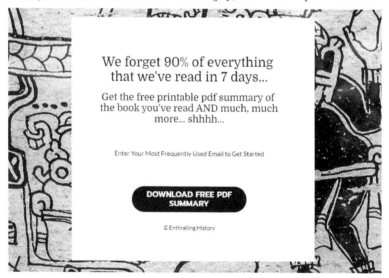

Table of Contents

Introduction

The Inca Empire was the biggest empire South America has ever seen. Tahuantinsuyu, the "land of the four quarters," stretched some 2,500 miles along the west coast of the continent from what is now Ecuador down to Chile at its height.

When most people think of the Inca, they think of Machu Picchu, the mountaintop city discovered by Hiram Bingham in 1911. But there was a lot more to the Inca Empire than that, and that's what this book sets out to explain.

What's amazing is that this empire was created in an incredibly unpromising environment. Unlike the Aztecs, who had the advantage of being based in one of the most fertile areas of Mesoamerica, the Inca inherited a land of steep mountains. The land had a short growing season and limited areas suitable for cultivation. The terrain is so difficult that just traveling twenty miles could take days. The Inca had no iron or horses. They never discovered the wheel and had no writing system, yet they built an immense empire.

And this empire grew from nothing in just fifty years. However, it only lasted one hundred years in total. While the Inca went back to 1200 CE or so, they were, for a long time, just one small tribe among others. Their rise to power was dramatically sudden, and their fall was just as dramatic. Even more amazing, there were possibly as few as forty thousand full-blooded Inca ruling over an empire of up to twelve million people.

This book will show the whole history of the Inca Empire, starting with how the Inca arose and ending with the struggle against the Spanish occupation. It will also talk about how the empire was organized and administered, the arts and crafts of the Inca, and the agricultural advances that made it possible to feed a growing population and, most importantly, supply the armies the empire needed for its conquests.

This comprehensive guide will also take a look at Inca society, which is very different from ours in the way it is organized, and at Inca religion. While the Inca had similar deities to other Andean peoples, they refined their religious ideology to support the empire's aims.

Inca history can be confusing. Hiram Bingham called it "a maze of doubt and contradictions." [1] The Inca did not have a writing system (at least, not in the way you would think), so our evidence for Inca history before the arrival of the Spanish comes from accounts that were written later. These may incorporate oral history traditions, myths, or eyewitness accounts, but they also include various biases from Spanish historians aiming to justify colonization or from various different Inca clans and factions. Other information includes colonial censuses, the military, religious beliefs, and tax records, but by the time most of this was being recorded, the Inca and other people of the empire had already been affected by cultural changes, and the Spanish didn't always differentiate between the Inca and subject peoples.

Another confusion is that "Inca" can mean either the Inca people or the Inca, their ruler. To minimize confusion, the ruler is referred to by the full title of Sapa Inca ("Unique Inca" or "Only Inca") in this book.

Some historians characterize Inca rulers as lazy, aggressive, or innovative because they have focused on a selected source that has a certain bias. This book will try to steer clear of these biases and clearly distinguish what is certain from possible interpretations. You should also note that dates before the Spanish occupation are always approximations.

Many names are similar, with many using words such as Yupanqui ("honorable") or Capac ("royal"). The fact that the Inca had separate

---

[1] Bingham, Hiram. *Inca Land: Explorations in the Highlands of Peru*. 2003.

childhood and adult names and, in the case of rulers, a separate regnal name can also be confusing. Yahuar Huacac ("blood weeper") was the nickname and regnal name of Titu Cusi Huallpa, and Atahualpa is known by his original name rather than his regnal name of Caccha Pachacuti Inca Yupanqui.

Spelling can also be an issue. The ruler Huayna Capac's name is also spelled Guayna Cápac, Guayna Capac, Huain Capac, Guain Capac, Guayana Capac, Wayna Kapa, Wayn Capac, Wayana Qhapaq, Wayna Kapak, Wayna Capac, and Wayna Qhapaq. In this book, the most common spelling will be used. (*Hu* is pronounced as a *w*, so Huacac is pronounced "wakak.")

This book also benefits from relatively recent research on the Inca and their world, using recent archaeological finds and ethnology (comparisons of Inca customs with those of modern Andean societies). The study of the Inca Empire is a relatively recent discipline. While the archaeology and history of the Greeks and Romans were well established by 1900, two of the foundational discoveries of the Inca were only made in the 20th century. Guamán Poma's thousand-page manuscript, with its illustrations of Inca life, was discovered in 1908, and Machu Picchu was discovered in 1911.

Even more recently, the mummies of sacrificed children have been found on mountain peaks, and a number of cemeteries have been found with large numbers of mummified bodies. The fine state of preservation of these bodies, together with the textiles and other artifacts associated with them, allows archaeologists to greatly expand our knowledge of Inca life and customs.

However, you don't need to worry about all the difficulties involved in Inca history. Continue to the next chapter, and you'll get a picture of how the Inca evolved, the history and customs of their empire, and the continuing Inca influence on South America today.

PART ONE: ORIGINS AND DEVELOPMENT

Chapter 1: The Andes before the Inca

The Inca liked to present their empire as the first and only true civilization of the Peruvian highlands. Before them, there were only barbarians. When Manco Cápac founded the Inca Empire, peace, prosperity, and civilization arrived in the Inca capital, Cuzco.

In fact, the more we learn about the prehistoric Andean region, the more we realize that the Inca were just the last in a series of civilizations. There were at least two major civilizations before them that rapidly expanded and then suddenly fragmented again. Archaeologists have defined a number of horizons and intermediate periods known as the Rowe-Lanning chronology.

Period	Dates	Cultures
Pre-ceramic Period	Up to 1800 BCE	
Initial Period	1800–900 BCE	
Early Horizon	900–200 BCE	Chavín, Paracas
Early Intermediate Period	200 BCE–600 CE	Moche, Nazca
Middle Horizon	600–1000 CE	Tihuanaco, Huari

Late Intermediate Period	1000–1438 CE	Chimú, Chancay
Late Horizon	1438–1532	Inca

The Chavín culture developed in the northern highlands of Peru around 1000 or 900 BCE. Chavín de Huántar, which may have been its capital, has been excavated, showing evidence of the use of drainage canals and irrigation, as well as the use of rock from different areas. The Chavín culture developed gold work, including the use of soldering. They also domesticated llamas, which were used as pack animals, for their wool, and for their meat.

The Chavín culture's anthropomorphic animal pottery shows snakes, eagles, cats, and other animals.

The Paracas culture began a little later than the Chavín. It is best known for a large cemetery called the Paracas Cavernas, which shows evidence of the heads of the deceased being taken out and later reburied, as well as the creation of "mummy bundles," which held the seated cadaver, clothing, ornaments, and weapons within the wrappings. This is the first evidence of a practice that would become important to the Inca. Like many other Andean cultures (though not the Inca), the Paracas practiced skull flattening, tying infants' heads to boards so that their skulls would grow into a certain shape.

Both the Paracas and Chavín cultures show evidence of sophisticated weaving techniques. It's clear that craft specialization had already begun with the Chavín culture, and this became more pronounced in later cultures.

Around 200 BCE, the Nazca civilization developed in the south of Peru. They intensively cultivated the narrow river valleys of the region and used irrigation, including underground aqueducts. Their villages were always situated above the valley on the arid, uncultivated land; the agricultural land was too precious to use for housing. They built pyramids at Cahuachi, their ceremonial center, and used enemy heads as trophies. (Ceremonial centers in the early period often served a large area of small communities and did not have a large resident population.) The Nazca also buried their dead as mummies bundled in textiles with a selection of grave goods.

The Nazca culture created the celebrated geoglyphs, huge rock patterns laid out in the desert.

The Moche culture inhabited the northern coast of Peru and probably consisted of a number of separate nations sharing a common culture rather than a single state. The Moche culture appears to have begun around 100 CE and lasted for six hundred years. Like the Nazca, they used irrigation systems to enable intensive agriculture. Their land was fertilized by guano (seabird excrement), which was taken from the coastal cliffs or offshore islands.

The Moche culture created highly distinctive, naturalistic, and lively ceramics showing scenes of life, including hunting, fishing, fighting, and a range of different sexual activities. They also had sophisticated goldwork. The Moche built pyramidal structures from adobe, such as the Huaca de la Luna near the modern city of Trujillo; there is extensive evidence of human sacrifice at this site.

The Middle Horizon period saw the emergence of two major cultures: Tihuanaco (Tiwanaku) and Huari (Wari).

The Tihuanaco culture was based on the southern shore of Lake Titicaca in modern Bolivia and had the most advanced building technology in South America so far. The Gate of the Sun, which was located near Lake Titicaca, was a gateway made out of a single, ten-ton monolith that was extensively carved. Stepped platforms and terraced platform mounds have also been found.

The Gate of the Sun at Tihuanaco.

The Tihuanaco developed a raised field system with ditches running between the fields. Terraces and artificial ponds were also used. By using these techniques, the Tihuanaco were able to reclaim large tracts of unused land around Lake Titicaca.

The Tihuanaco appear to have been linked with the Huari culture, which covered much of the highlands and coasts of Peru.

The Huari introduced terracing to the Andes, which allowed for an increase in the variety of crops. Later, they added the former Moche area to their territories. They also created an early road system, though it was not quite as developed as the Inca Royal Road system would later become.

The Huari, like the Inca, used the quipu or knotted cord to record data. They shared the Staff God, a deity, with the Tihuanaco and practiced animal sacrifice (there is also evidence of human heads placed as offerings at one of their temples). While their architecture was not as highly developed as the Tihuanaco, their textiles are splendid. They are highly standardized and tend to use abstract designs. Like earlier cultures, the Huari made mummy bundles from their dead.

It is likely that both the Tihuanaco and the Huari collapsed because of major changes in the climate, which made their marginal agricultural output no longer viable and caused widespread famine.

All of these cultures are quite distinct, but they share a number of common features. There is a continuum of religious thought and social customs on which they all draw. Mummification (artificial or natural) and the burial of corpses in a seated position are common to most of them. They are most likely linked to a form of ancestor worship and to the idea that the dead were still involved in the world and could be used as guardians, oracles, or advisors.

A number of these cultures built mounds or pyramids, and the worship of natural features, such as mountain peaks, springs, and lakes, is evident.

Technologically, textile fabrication achieved a high level of sophistication. We know this because of the mummy bundles and the arid climate of the coast, which kept much evidence intact. Metalworking was also sophisticated, but ceramics generally seemed to be the most different between cultures.

It's also worth noting that many of these cultures achieved significant scale. They also built major monuments for religious and funerary purposes, whether in adobe (on the coast) or in stone (for instance, at Tihuanaco).

Chapter 2: The Founding of Cuzco

Looking at these cultures, you can see that the Inca entered the scene quite late; they are estimated to have arrived at Cuzco (also spelled as Cusco) around 1200. That's 2,100 years or so after the Chavín culture—as far away as we are now from the Roman Empire. (The likely date of the Incas' arrival does not come not from Inca oral sources but from artifacts found near Cuzco.)

The Upper Huatanay Valley already counted several different peoples living around the Cuzco area. There were two reasons for this. First, a large area of relatively flat land was attractive, as it was easily cultivated, and secondly, the Huatanay crossing made it a natural trading center. The indigenous Huallas, Sauasiray incomers, Alcavizas, and Antasaya all lived in what appears to have been a loose confederation. It was an unusual concentration of people for the Andes, which was generally sparsely inhabited.

And then Manco Cápac arrived.

* * *

Manco Cápac *might* actually be a myth. Just as the Romans had Romulus and Remus and England had King Arthur, Manco Cápac may have been a later invention; certainly, much of the early history of Cuzco is mythical.

There are not one but two creation myths for Cuzco. In the first, Manco Cápac came out of a mountain cave at Pacaritambo with his three brothers and four sisters and made his way to Cuzco. Ayar Cachi was too ferocious, and the other three brothers walled him up in the cave. Ayar Uchu, the second brother, became a sacred stone on Huanacauri Mountain, which was later used for male puberty rituals by the Inca. And Ayar Auca became a stone guardian for the meadows near Cuzco, leaving Manco Cápac alone with his sisters (and wives). Manco Cápac founded a new city and became the first Sapa Inca.

Burr Cartwright Brundage, a professor of history, believes the four brothers might represent the diverse peoples at the origin of the Inca state.[2] The cave origin myth is found in the stories of other Andean peoples too, though their caves are in different sites; it seems to have been commonplace. Caves were always regarded as *huacas* or sacred sites or objects.

However, there is a second origin myth for the Inca in which Manco Cápac and his sister-wife, Mama Ocllo, emerge from the waters of Lake Titicaca. This looks like an attempt by the Inca to square the circle after the expansion to the south that took place under Topa Inca. (At the same time, the Inca appear to have rearranged the existing cult of the mother goddess and mountain-cat god on the islands of the lake into a cult of Inti and Mama Quilla, the Inca sun god and moon mother, respectively.)

No wonder early Inca history has been referred to as "runic uncertainties!"[3] What we do know is that Cuzco is the oldest continuously inhabited city in South America. Even today, you can see Spanish houses built on massive Inca stone foundations and the huge masonry walls of Coricancha (a temple) underneath the Convent of Santo Domingo.

It's likely that the Inca immigrated from the Urubamba Valley, north of Cuzco. They originally may have been a raiding, semi-nomadic people that eventually settled in Cuzco. They took over three of the existing tribes there, but the Alcavizas remained

---

[2] Brundage, Burr Cartwright. *Empire of the Inca (The Civilization of the American Indian Series)*. University of Oklahoma Press, Norman, 1963, pg. 18.

[3] Brundage, Burr Cartwright. *Empire of the Inca*. Pg. 23.

independent. Though they were eventually absorbed, Pachacuti, a Sapa Inca, evidently didn't trust them since he expelled them to the suburbs.

The scale of Cuzco at this point was small. The initial Inca conquests were of villages consisting of a few hundred people. There were just three or four miles between them. Manco Cápac's Cuzco had a population of well under a thousand. It was a tiny city-state not very different from others in the region, and the Intihuasi, or the house of the sun god (the site of the later Coricancha), was just a small courtyard with adobe-thatched buildings.

The leader originally was a war leader, or *sinchi*, and it's clear from the name of Manco Cápac's son and successor, Sinchi Roca, that this was still the case. He appears to have come to the throne around 1230 and ruled for about thirty years. Under his rule, the development of Cuzco continued. The amount of land under cultivation was increased, mainly by draining the marshes at the bottom of the river valleys.

Sinchi Rocha's successor as Sapa Inca was Lloque Yupanqui. There is not a great deal known about him, and some historians have described him as lazy and cowardly. However, negative elements in Inca history may come from opposing Inca factions. Lloque Yupanqui appears to have created the *acllahuasi* ("house of the chosen ones," similar to a convent for women) and started road building. The bureaucracy with hereditary *curacas* (magistrates) may have also been created around this time.

The next ruler, Mayta Cápac, is interesting. His story feels like a return to the country of myth. He is said to have been born with teeth, and at two years old, he could fight much older warriors and win. He inherited the throne around 1290, and his figure is celebrated in Inca legend, as he expresses the aggressiveness and fighting spirit of the Inca Empire.

Mayta Cápac is also said to have created the cult of Inti, making Manco Cápac's personal fetish of the sun-falcon into the center of a national cult. This was crucial for the creation of the empire since it gave the Inca a religious ideology of their own, making their ruling house divine as sons of the sun and letting them feel superiority over other peoples.

Cápac Yupanqui was probably the first Sapa Inca to take his people outside the immediate neighborhood of Cuzco, raiding in the Yucay Valley. He moved from *hurin* Cuzco (lower Cuzco, around Coricancha) to *hanan* Cuzco (upper Cuzco) but gave Coricancha to his brother, the high priest, keeping control within the royal clan.

Cápac Yupanqui's successor was Inca Roca, who married Mama Micay from the Yucay Valley. Her family is said to have introduced irrigation, and it was during this period that the drainage and irrigation of the lands around Cuzco were improved. Inca Roca is also said to have established the *yachayhuasi*, the schools for Inca youth and the sons of provincial *curacas*. It is probably around this date that some of the surrounding people were given the status of Inca by adoption.

Yahuar Huacac, "blood weeper," got his name when he was abducted as a child by an Ayamarca warlord. He wept tears of blood. When the Ayamarca leader saw this, he decided he could not take the risk of killing the boy since he was clearly divine in some way. Eventually, Yahuar Huacac escaped back to Cuzco. Inca Roca was later prevailed on to give the Ayamarcas the status of Inca by privilege. Yahuar Huacac also married an Ayamarca coya (a coya is a queen), so it seems that despite the apparently violent nature of the episode from his childhood, a diplomatic arrangement had been reached, and a rapprochement between the two peoples had taken place.

By this point, Cuzco would have had a population of around four thousand or five thousand, only a quarter of which would have been men of fighting age. Given the need for some men to work the fields and the fact some priests were tied to the temple, it is believed the Inca army during this period would have numbered only 250 to 500 men. (The Boston Tea Party was the work of about 130 men, according to some accounts; they would have made up half an Inca army!)

With Viracocha, who succeeded Yahuar Huacac around 1410, historical information becomes more trustworthy. The Inca would leave the world of myth and enter more concrete history.

A handy guide to the early Sapa Incas

Manco Cápac	Mythical? c. 1200
Sinchi Roca	1230-1260
Lloque Yupanqui	1260-1290
Mayta Cápac	1290-1320
Cápac Yupanqui	1320-1350
Inca Roca	1350-1380
Yahuar Huacac	1380-1410
Viracocha Inca / Hatun Topa Inca	1410-1438
Pachacuti Inca	1438-1471

Note that the first Sapa Incas did not carry "Inca" as part of their names; it's only from Viracocha's time on that this became standard. This was also about the same time that the Inca started to build an empire rather than a small nation. It may also represent a change from the original elective warlord status of the Sapa Inca (as indicated by Sinchi Roca's name) to the hereditary principle.

Viracocha was likely the first Sapa Inca who actually ruled Inca conquests on a permanent basis, introducing administration through tribute, a labor tax, and the installation of Inca governors. Previously, the Inca had raided, looted, or made alliances; Viracocha started to integrate the conquered territories. It is likely that the foundations of the Inca administrative machine were laid under Viracocha, though Pachacuti perfected the system.

Viracocha appears to have been quite successful in the earlier part of his reign, but he eventually was faced with a challenge to which he was not equal. When the Chancas, who inhabited the region of Ayacucho and Apurímac, attacked Cuzco, Viracocha fled the city with his chosen heir, Inca Urco. His third son, Cusi Inca Yupanqui, stayed in Cuzco and successfully defended the city. There are various accounts of exactly how things happened, but Cusi Inca Yupanqui ended up in control, taking the name Pachacuti Inca or "Earth Shaker."

The Inca believed that time ran in cycles, with each era ending with an earthquake or dramatic change. So, by taking this name, Pachacuti was promising a new era, one that was completely different from the past. Pachacuti's accession in 1438 is often taken as the effective date that the Inca Empire began.

The Chancas' aggression may have been one of the determining factors that forced the Inca to grow up fast and create an empire rather than staying a small, if fairly feisty, tribe. The Inca had been expanding their territory slowly and successfully, but the next three generations would see their expansion supercharged, as they took huge swathes of new territory.

Pachacuti certainly saw and took the opportunity that lay before him, creating his own powerful myths in the process. He had a vision granted to him by the god Inti. He saw the future in a magic mirror. And as the Chancas descended on Cuzco, the very stones in the fields turned themselves into warriors fighting on Pachacuti's side. (This myth has great resonance with the Inca creation myth since the stones were clearly *huacas*, like the brothers of Manco Cápac who had turned into stone guardians.) Perhaps by claiming to have a vision from Inti, Pachacuti was deliberately turning his back on the god after which his father was named, Viracocha the creator.

It's said that Pachacuti publicly insulted his father when Viracocha returned to Cuzco, making him drink chicha (similar to kombucha) from a filthy jar and calling him a cowardly woman. When the enemy chieftains were presented so that Viracocha could step on their necks, which was part of the Inca victory ritual, Pachacuti would not allow his father to do it. He insisted on treading on the enemies himself. This humiliation was unprecedented. Viracocha retired to his estates, and he appears to have died shortly after.

Pachacuti re-founded Cuzco, extensively rebuilding it around 1440. He set about the creation of an empire, and he was greatly helped by the fact that the Chancas were now serving in the Inca army, vastly increasing its size.

* * *

Pachacuti's rebuilding of Cuzco wasn't just architectural; he actually changed the shape of the landscape. He redirected the two rivers, the Huatanay and Tullumayo, to run parallel on either side of the city center and enclosed them in stone banks. Sections of the Huatanay were even paved. Pachacuti envisaged the city as a puma, with its head at the peak of Sacsahuamán (a citadel) and its tail represented by the merged rivers after their confluence. In the belly was the great plaza, mirrored by another plaza south of the river: Haucaypata (the great plaza), where festivals were celebrated, and Cusipata, where military parades were held. The *ushna*, a dais for the Sapa Inca, was built in the center of Haucaypata.

The city was divided into two moieties (or halves), upper and lower Cuzco, and the interior of the city was built on a grid plan, with four arterial roads running to the four quarters. The city was also divided into ten canchas or compounds (the division of space or social structures by two and then by ten seems to have been a typical Inca trait, using division into pairs within a decimal system). Adobe houses were replaced by stone palaces and houses, though Cuzco retained its thatched roofs.

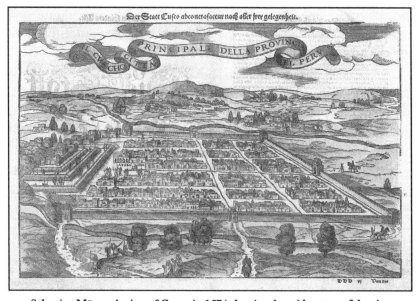

Sebastian Münster's view of Cuzco in 1574 showing the grid system of the city.

The palaces were now clustered around Haucaypata. Pachacuti's palace, Condorcancha, was built to match Viracocha's Hatuncancha, and the *yachayhuasi* (schools for noble Inca and the sons of *curacas*) were also located here. It was from this plaza that all executive, administrative, and religious functions were exercised. All of the later palaces had entrances to the main square, and nearby was the acllahuasi, where the chosen women lived and learned how to weave and make chicha. (Today, the site houses a convent.)

Pachacuti also rebuilt Inticancha, renaming it Coricancha (the "gold compound"), the original kernel of the city. A new golden image of the sun god was personally set in place by the Sapa Inca. A golden egg on one altar was set between a silver moon and a golden sun, representing Viracocha between Inti and Mama Quilla. The mummies of former Sapa Incas were arranged on platforms against the wall of the temple, and their *coyas* (queens) were in another building devoted to the moon goddess. Coricancha's walls were plated with gold, and gold wire was woven into the thatch.

Only the noble Incas lived in the center of the city. Outside the grid, Cuzco was arranged differently, forming a hub-and-spoke structure with lines radiating out. A ring of agricultural lands surrounded the center before the suburbs were reached. Storehouses were placed on the hills around the city.

The *ceque* system of lines radiating from Coricancha was not only a design but also a sacred diagram connecting 385 *huacas*, of which 328 created the calendar; each of these *huacas* had a day of the year. It can be compared to a quipu; each line is a quipu string, while each *huaca* is a knot. So, Cuzco was, in a way, a giant quipu that recorded the rites and ceremonies of the Inca.

Cuzco was a tightly controlled city. There were checkpoints; no one could enter between sunset and sunrise. Visitors from outlying provinces were obliged to occupy the quarter that corresponded to their province. If they came from Quito, they had to occupy the northeastern quarter, and since they wore their local clothing, it was easy to make sure they were in the right place. Cuzco was also a holy city, a sort of Inca Vatican. It encapsulated the sacred nature of the Sapa Inca, his predecessors, and the history of the empire. Items from *huacas* and idols that were taken from subject peoples were held hostage in Cuzco.

Cuzco continued to grow and become wealthier and more elegant after Pachacuti's rebuilding. When the Spanish arrived, they were impressed by the city, as they had never seen anything like it.

* * *

Viracocha laid the foundations, but Pachacuti created the empire. At least, that is what Inca history says. However, we know that Pachacuti rewrote history, although perhaps a better word is "re-represented," as Inca history was told through a series of pictures painted on tablets as mnemonic prompts for the oral history memorized by Inca historians. Although the Inca were preliterate, calling them "prehistoric" is not accurate since they had a highly developed sense of history and many non-alphabetic ways of ensuring its transmission.

Pachacuti opened the way to the greater world. When he took Ollantaytambo, he gave the Inca command of two out of three routes into the Sacred Valley (Urubamba Valley). And by securing Vilcabamba, he gave them access to the eastern side of the Andes. They were no longer imprisoned in a little pocket of the valley.

Pachacuti appears to have started or at least dramatically increased the use of the *mitma* system of moving subject peoples around the empire. These deportations were normal from this period onward. For instance, a tribe that rebelled might be moved into a settled and loyal province where they could not foment trouble. Sometimes, Inca were moved to settle in new provinces and provide a base of loyal administrators. Craftspeople were often moved into Cuzco, creating a form of technology transfer with new expert weavers and metalworkers. The movement of different tribes had another benefit too; it helped to diffuse Quechua as the lingua franca.

Pachacuti could be ruthless as a commander. He sent his younger brother, Cápac Inca Yupanqui, north but told him not to proceed beyond the Yanamyo or Black River. That was sensible since the area was not completely pacified, and the army could easily be cut off if any trouble started.

However, Cápac Inca Yupanqui headed into enemy Cajamarca, finding it just too tempting a target. On hearing of this move, Pachacuti ordered Cápac Inca Yupanqui to be killed along with another brother, Huayna Yupanqui, who had gone on the same campaign. Disobeying the Sapa Inca carried a capital sentence, even if it involved the Sapa Inca's brother. But Pachacuti did take hold of Cajamarca, which turned out to be quite important for later expansion in the north.

Viracocha had been a warlord; Pachacuti was an emperor. His accession in 1438 is when most historians date the real start of the Inca Empire.

The next few chapters of this book will look at the empire's administration, agriculture, crafts, and religion before picking up the chronological history again.

PART TWO: INCA SOCIAL LIFE AND POLITICS

Chapter 3: Political Organization, Laws, and Administration

The real miracle of the Inca is not the fact they were able to conquer such diverse and expansive territories but that they were able to integrate them into a single structure. The Inca may have been helped by the fact that many of the subject peoples had fairly similar cultures, and they tended to build on those existing political and social structures rather than replace them. Conquered peoples would work on behalf of the state, generally doing the same jobs that they had already been doing, and the empire provided security and infrastructure in return. So, it's important to keep in mind the division of the Inca and their subject peoples. Only the minority of the Inca Empire was made up of Inca, and they had a very different status from that of non-Inca subjects.

The empire's political organization has been described as "socialist" by Louis Baudin, a social scientist. The empire blended social, religious, and ritual aspects in a single ideology. It was, in many ways, a highly rational plan for the organization of a society in which every subject should have a sufficient amount of food and goods, with taxes paying for the upkeep of the administration. There was no real concept of private property; in theory, all land belonged to the state or, rather, to the Sapa Inca. There were various state monopolies:

coca, captives, the *acllahuasi*, state pastures for guanacos and vicuñas (both related to the llama), and the mining of precious metals.[4]

However, Inca society was very class-based and class-conscious, which is not typical of socialism. It was also entirely subject to the authority of the Sapa Inca, whose will was law. And since the Sapa Inca was the son of Inti, the law was based on religious rights, so any violation of the law was sacrilege. Attempting to assimilate the Inca Empire to any scheme of Western thought is fraught with danger.

Land was held by the Sapa Inca (whether the current ruler or a *panaca*, the household of a former king), by the religious establishment, or by an *ayllu* (clan); it might even be held by a *huaca*. Ownership is difficult to discuss since the system of tenure appears to have been somewhat mixed. The Spanish latched on to the idea that all land belonged to the Sapa Inca personally, but this was at least partly motivated by the neat legal fiction that the last Sapa Inca passed his possessions to the king of Spain. This enabled the Spanish to sidestep all indigenous claims to the land.

In fact, documentary evidence of ownership claims in the colonial period, often through Inca women who married Spanish husbands, shows that it was not quite so simple. Perhaps the closest analogy would be the way many countries administer mineral rights; they claim state ownership but allow private organizations to extract the minerals in exchange for payment of royalties.

Village land for cultivation would be divided into three parts: the sun, the Sapa Inca, and the village. The villagers would cultivate all three parts of the land, living off what they produced on their third while sending the rest of the produce as tribute. While, in theory, the split was by thirds, the land given to an *ayllu* was probably planned to be enough for self-sufficiency for the remainder of the land to be divided between the Sapa Inca and the gods. Thus, the proportions would reflect the type and fertility of the land. Taxes were taken in the form of labor or the production of that labor.

This arrangement grew out of Andean culture, in which land was usually cultivated by the village or clan in cooperation, but it was changed by Pachacuti, who regularized a bureaucracy and the *mitma*

---

[4] Baudin, Louis. *A Socialist Empire: The Inca of Peru.* D Van Nostrand, Princeton, 1961.

system to exploit it better.

However, the increasing class consciousness of the empire was a move away from the roughly egalitarian Andean culture. The earliest Sapa Incas appear to have been elected, but over time, there was a move toward a system of blood inheritance. The rules were strict: only the sons of the Sapa Inca and the coya were eligible, not sons of a concubine. The Sapa Inca had to marry one of his full sisters to keep the royal blood pure. (Brother/sister relationships were prohibited for everyone apart from the Sapa Inca, though the marriage of first cousins was common.)

There still appears to have been an element of assent required, as after Pachacuti, the Sapa Inca generally indicated who he wished to be his heir. Co-rulership occurred in a number of cases. However, the oldest son of the Sapa Inca was not always chosen, and occasionally, the Sapa Inca's choice was ruled inadmissible.

The Sapa Inca wore the *Mascapaicha* or crown of red with tassels attached to his headband as a symbol of royalty. Above this were two or three black and white feathers; the whole thing was secured by a headband wrapped several times around the head.

No one could look the Sapa Inca in the face, and those who entered his presence for the first time had to come barefoot, bearing a burden. Increasing mystery and awe surrounded the person of the Sapa Inca. Although the Inca ruler was initially a warlord, the rulers eventually became godlike and remote.

The Inca were exempt from manual labor. The Inca also had the privilege of wearing ear spools or ear plugs that enlarged their ear lobes. The Spanish called them *orejones* or "big ears." Inca were also subject to different laws and different criminal punishments than subject peoples. They could also confess privately to Inti. Subject peoples had to confess publicly. In many cases, public confession appears to have been used as a way of gaining information about political discontent or encouraging subjects to report on the wrongdoing of their neighbors. Effectively, the Inca had the privilege of privacy.

There were further class divisions within the Inca. There were eleven *ayllus* (clans) of Inca of royal blood and ten of non-royal Inca. There were also the Inca by privilege, who were assimilated over time to boost the numbers needed to manage the empire. They could not live in the center of Cuzco. However, they were still crucial for expansion, as they formed a class of administrators and colonists.

A set of sumptuary laws set down what each class of Inca was allowed to wear. There were even laws on what foods they could eat. Social mobility was extremely limited, though the army allowed individuals to rise to a higher class based on their performance as warriors.

The empire was divided into four regions or *suyus*. Its Inca name was Tahuantinsuyu, the land of the four quarters.

Chinchaysuyu	North
Antisuyu	East
Collasuyu	South
Cuntisuyu	West

The household was the basic unit of accounting, not the individual. In theory, twenty thousand households made up a province. Each quarter was divided into several provinces.

Government structures were hierarchical and reflected the way the Inca divided things into twos, fours, and tens. There were four apus (governors), each in charge of a "quarter." They had eighty provincial governors under them.

Each province was then divided into two halves, each with a *curaca* (magistrate) looking after ten thousand households. Each *curaca* had ten *huarancas* reporting to him, with each looking after one thousand households. Further divisions were applied all the way down to the *chunca-camayu*, who looked after a mere ten households.

Some of these numbers are probably inexact and may have been made up by *mitma* labor. It is also possible the disparities were simply ignored. However, it is clear to see that the hierarchical chain of command allowed Cuzco to have unprecedented control of its resources in the provinces. Records were taken at each level and sent to the capital on a quipu. This allowed labor to be distributed throughout the population, for instance, for road building, and it allowed agricultural and other products to be sent where they were needed. It was a simple but powerful system.

A table of Inca organization

Inca name	English equivalent	Number of households
Apu	Viceroy	Head of a "quarter" of the empire
Tucricuc ("he who sees all")	Provincial governor	20,000
Hunu-camayu	Deputy governor	10,000
Huaranca	Head of a thousand	1,000
Pachaca-camayu	Captain	500
Picha-camayu	Centurion	100
Picha-chunca-camayu	Superior decurion	50
Chunca-camayu	Decurion	10

The economy was not based on money, and there was no inter-regional trading. The empire was based on blending the Andean subsistence and self-sufficient economies that preceded it with the distribution of surpluses. The production and distribution of all commodities were organized by the government, though some local markets were tolerated.

The quipu was a major aid for the Inca. It was made of a single string to which other threads of different colors were attached in sequence. On these threads, knots were made in particular places to show numbers. For instance, the quipu was used to take censuses of the population, to show the division of age groups, and to report the llama population.

The different colors of thread showed the type of data being related: black for time, red for the Sapa Inca, yellow for gold, and blue for religion. This system of references had to be memorized by quipu users so they could interpret the numerical information. The "keepers of memory" in Cuzco were exempt from paying taxes and were highly valued; the Sapa Inca paid their living expenses. Without them, the quipus were just many bits of string. When Atahualpa wanted to wipe out the memories of his brother Huáscar, he had the memory keepers slaughtered and destroyed the quipus.

Some archaeologists now think the quipu may have been capable of showing more detailed and unstructured information than was previously thought. They might even have represented a basic stage of literacy. However, no one has yet managed to come up with a definitive reading of a quipu.

It might also be problematic that most of the quipus that survive have been found in tombs. It's unlikely that these would be quipus dealing with state census information; they might represent prayers or recount the individual's life story.

A quipu in the Machu Picchu Museum.

Pi3.124, CC BY-SA 4.0 <https://creativecommons.org/licenses/by-sa/4.0>, via Wikimedia Commons
https://commons.wikimedia.org/wiki/File:Quipo_in_the_Museo_Machu_Picchu,_Casa_Concha,_Cusco.jpg

One of the difficulties with arriving at firm dates for Inca history is related to the quipu since the Inca added activities and durations. They might say, for instance, "This conquest took five years, then two years were taken to subdue this city," instead of saying, "The conquest took until 1445, then in 1447, this city was subdued." The Inca way of remembering history is a kind of sequence, and adding that would have been done on a quipu instead of, as we do, numbering each year, and it is the way some early chroniclers, like Betanzos, presented their history. Other Spanish writers may have heard similar things from Inca informants and tried to assign firm dates, so the dates they give cannot necessarily be trusted. Needless to say, this creates a great deal of uncertainty.

The quipu survives today, though in a much simpler form. Shepherds in the Central Andean puna still use knotted strings to count their animals.

The judicial system in the Inca Empire was the same as the administrative system; there were no separate judges. A number of offenses were punishable by death, including adultery, theft, murder, and treason. There were no prisons. Other punishments included mutilation or having a boulder dropped on one's back. The Inca also appear to have practiced a form of "three strikes, and you're out," with different punishments for the first, second, and third offenses of the same kind of crime.

Theft was punished if it was motivated by greed or envy. However, if someone stole because they needed to, for instance, in order to eat, the official in charge of their village would be punished for failing to ensure they had sufficient means of sustenance. The empire regulated the lives of its subjects extremely tightly, but it also ensured they received everything necessary—a form of reciprocity that is rooted in Andean customs.

The Inca had a magnificent system of logistics. They built not only an extensive road system but also rest houses and storehouses along the roads at regular distances. There was a tambo (rest house) roughly every day's journey. By using the storehouses (*colca*), supplies could be sent to any part of the empire using llama caravans or human carriers.

Llamas can carry up to eighty pounds on steep slopes. They have great endurance and can forage for their own food, so nothing has to be supplied for them. They are highly efficient creatures except for one limitation; they cannot be ridden.

The Inca responded to this limitation by creating a relay system of messengers who lived at roughly one-mile distances along the roads. They could run messages and quipus quickly. A messenger ran his mile and then handed his message to the next messenger while still running. Each messenger was fresh at the start of his journey, so they could run much faster than a man who needed to run a longer distance.

An example of the speed at which communication could be handled is the fact that it took three days for a message taken by the *chasquis* (messengers) to reach Cuzco from Lima, which was roughly 150 miles. In the colonial era, the mail service over the same distance took twelve to thirteen days by horse.

The roads also enabled the army to move quickly and efficiently to any part of the empire by using the system of storehouses to supply the men. This greatly simplified military logistics and was a key enabler of Inca expansion.

Inca and Subject Peoples

In the imperial period, the Inca did not try to integrate subject peoples in terms of religion. Subject tribes kept their own gods and many of their own customs, including their own forms of burial rites. However, they were integrated into the *ayllu* system and into the bureaucracy of the empire, which used divisions of two (as the moieties) and ten—a fully decimal system that put mathematics ahead of practicality.

Indeed, subject peoples were legally obliged to wear their tribal costume and hairstyle or head covering so that they could easily be identified and so that they could not be confused with true Incas.

However, the sons of local rulers and administrators were educated in the *yachayhuasi*, or house of learning, in Cuzco alongside the young Inca nobles. They learned Quechua, Inca history, and how to administer the Inca bureaucracy. They became thoroughly indoctrinated in the Inca way of life. Quechua became the common language of the empire, creating a sense of common culture and simplifying administrative processes.

The *mitma* system also helped to create a common culture by allowing the deportation of people groups to different parts of the empire. There, they would have lost their local *huacas* and might not be able to speak their own language to the other inhabitants, so Quechua would be needed for their successful integration.

Some farmers were moved from one climatic zone to another to transfer their knowledge and the species they knew how to grow. This must have had a significant impact on agricultural productivity.

The *mitma* system also worked on an individual basis. For instance, skilled practitioners of crafts might be moved to Cuzco to work for the royal household or the temple, where they would provide craftwork of high quality. In some cases, this appears to have been a form of technology transfer, allowing the Inca to benefit from metallurgical or textile expertise that they did not originally have.

Labor Tax

Garcilaso de la Vega, an Inca by birth though he wrote after spending years in Spain, said that the laws of the Inca were simple. They were *ama sua, ama llulla,* and *ama quella*: do not steal, do not lie, and do not be lazy. Idleness was something that was not allowed in the Inca Empire unless, of course, you were an Inca noble, in which case, apart from warfare, it was obligatory.

Inca administration and Andean mores were highly prescriptive. Doing too little work was punished. Doing too much was also wrong, as it would enable someone else to do too little. Though this applied to the *ayllu* system, under which all of the clan households were responsible for the well-being of the community, the Inca also created a system under which labor was also used as a tax payment.

This was organized so that only a small number of adult men from each community was taken at any one time, allowing the *ayllu* to support itself and pay its tribute. For instance, a new bridge might need six hundred men over eighteen months. If that was split over the two moieties of a province, each half would need to find three hundred men; that meant thirty men from each one-thousand-household division or three men out of one hundred households. They also worked on rotation so that each man was not absent from home for more than a few months. While the new bridge probably was not the only project that needed to be done, it illustrates how the system was able to support the huge Inca investment in infrastructure without placing undue strain on the population by delegating human resources down through the *curaca* system.

Apart from tribute and the labor tax, the life of many *ayllus* did not change markedly in the early years of the empire. (Later, it appears that corvée labor became a much greater imposition, with people having to do more and more work.) People cultivated the same land in the same way they always had by sending some products to state storehouses. Occasionally, individuals would be called on to work on state projects or join the army. By and large, life under the Inca was the same as life before the Inca.

However, one form of tax that must have been very unpopular was the taking of *aclla* or "chosen women." Girls were taken at ages seven to twelve for training. When they were taken, they became the exclusive property of the Inca and ceased to belong to their birth *ayllu*. They would be taken to an *acllahuasi*, where they would be trained for four years in weaving, the making of chicha, and religion. It is unlikely that they ever saw their birth families or villages again.

At around fourteen or fifteen, the girls were divided into those who would become the Incas' concubines, those who would serve the gods (either by being sacrificed or serving as *mamacona*, a type of priestess), and those who could be used as rewards for warriors and administrators (basically a state treasury of available women). Some were also trained as singers. While the main *acllahuasi* was in Cuzco, there were up to forty separate establishments in the empire. They must have represented a significant part of textile production, particularly of the high-quality cumbi cloth.

* * *

One special and quite strange feature of the Inca Empire was the fact that the ruler never died. In most Andean cultures, the dead were considered to be effectively gone, although they occupied a different level of existence. For instance, mummies could give advice or influence the weather. This applied particularly to the Sapa Inca, whose mummy would be kept in Coricancha. It would be regularly fed and even visited from time to time by his father's or son's mummy for after-death socializing.

Inca mummies were not like Egyptian mummies. The Inca were put in a seated position as if they were still alive, with their knees drawn up to their chins and wrapped in textiles. Although some people refer to this as the fetal position, the mummies were always seated and not buried on their sides. They may have been completely and extensively wrapped. Archaeologists often refer to them as "mummy bundles," some of which contained more than one body, but they were never put in a sarcophagus. The Sapa Inca mummies wore royal regalia and were made to look just as they did when alive. They must have looked quite splendid when they were all lined up in the main square.

Split inheritance laws allowed all the Sapa Incas' sons *except* the next Sapa Inca to inherit his property jointly. It was still, so to speak, owned by the dead Sapa Inca and was administered by his relatives. This created a special form of the *ayllu* called a *panaca*, a "kingdom within a kingdom."5 Its job was to manage the estate and maintain the king's cult by "feeding" and making sacrifices to the mummy. The Sapa Inca's story would also be passed down in the *panaca*, often by reciting it in front of the mummy to remind him of his life.

Split inheritance was not unique to the Inca. It was also known in Chimor (home of the Chimú), which had a similar mummy cult. The capital, Chan Chan, had a series of palaces, with each one becoming the tomb of its king after his death. While the earlier palaces seem to have held a number of mummies, perhaps four or five generations worth, later palaces appear to have held only one, suggesting an intensification of the strictness of the rules. (Of course, this would have also made the practice more costly.)

The Sapa Inca created his *panaca* in a number of ways. From the day he took power, he would be concerned with building his future life as a mummy. First, he would build a new palace in Cuzco since he couldn't live in his father's palace anymore. He might also build estates in the country; these were part hunting lodges, part agricultural estates, and part pleasure resorts. A Sapa Inca might own a number of estates. The Yucay Valley was a particularly popular place for building such royal properties. In fact, Machu Picchu is likely to have been a royal estate rather than a fortress. Each estate was self-sufficient and staffed by *yanaconas* (servants).

---

5 Conrad, Geoffrey & Demarest, Arthur A. *Religion and Empire: The Dynamics of Aztec and Inca Expansionism.* Cambridge University Press, 1984. Pg. 131.

The mummy of a Sapa Inca being carried on a litter drawn by Guamán Poma de Ayala.
https://commons.wikimedia.org/wiki/File:Momia_Inca_-_Guaman_Poma_de_Ayala.jpg

Politically, this had an intriguing result: much of the nobility owed their loyalty to a dead Inca, not to the current one since they belonged to a former Inca's *panaca*. This led to increased factionalism among the Inca nobles.

But there was a more serious result too. Since the new Sapa Inca inherited nothing except the title from his father, he needed to conquer new lands or reclaim land for agriculture and build his own palace. This created a dynamic of conquest that could not be switched off. As the number of *panacas* and the size of the empire increased, each new Sapa Inca had to look further and further for land.

Ruler	Panaca
Manco Cápac	Chima - red
Sinchi Roca	Raura - fire
Lloque Yupanqui	Ahuayni - grandchild
Mayta Cápac	Usca Mayta - Captain Mayta
Cápac Yupanqui	Apu Mayta - beggar Mayta
Inca Roca	Vicaquirau - Vica cradle
Yahuar Huacac	Aucaylli - song of triumph
Viracocha	Socso - debility
Pachacuti Inca Yupanqui	Iñaca - mantle
Topa Inca Yupanqui	Capac - magnificent
Huayna Capac	Tomebamba (after the city in the north)
Huáscar Inca	Huáscar
Atahualpa	None

Although the Cuzco *panacas* came to an end with Huáscar (Atahualpa didn't have enough time to create one), the Neo-Inca rulers continued the tradition and the veneration of mummies. Tupac Amaru, the last Sapa Inca, was said to have been made guardian of his father, Manco Inca's, mummy by Inca Titu Cusi, his brother, which was a typical appointment for a member of the royal family. (Often, it was a way of keeping potential rivals out of the way.) We also know that the Spanish took the mummies of Manco Inca and Titu Cusi when they captured Tupac Amaru. They later destroyed the mummies.

Chapter 4: Inca Agriculture

The Inca Empire covered a huge north-south slice of South America. It had three different environmental strips: coastal desert, with arid lands separated by river valley oases; highlands; and eastern foothills descending to the Amazon rainforest. It was (and still is) a land of violent contrasts and dramatic weather.

The highlands were also divided into three separate zones, depending on the height of the land. These zones were the yunga, the lowest region, which was relatively warm and dry and where fruit trees could flourish; the quechua, where crops, such as corn, beans, squash, and quinoa, could be grown; and the puna, which was cold and wet. Only tubers like potatoes and oca grew well in the puna, but it provided excellent pasture for llamas and alpacas.

The whole region is unhospitable; there are very sudden steep rises, and the river valley bottoms, which would otherwise make good land for cultivation, are unusable because they flood. There is little rain because the prevailing winds blow from the east, letting moisture fall on the eastern side of the Andes. All of the indigenous cultures in this region began in small pockets of productive land: the river valleys on the coast and basins such as Cuzco or the Yucay Valley inland. Elsewhere, there was simply no way to sustain such a large population.

However, from Tihuanaco onward, good administration and investment in agricultural technology led to excellent productivity. Terraces, the use of fertilizer, the creation of a raised bed system, and the development of better crops through selective breeding transformed the people's hard-scrabble existence into a more stable existence. The Inca added an excellent empire-wide system of storage for surpluses. This moved them from a subsistence farming society, which was prone to famines in poor years, to a much more stable society in which the state held up to seven years' supply.

In the highlands, there were two main farming systems: *ayllu* and *mink'a*. The *ayllu* cultivated its land as a community; most Andean farmers still do. Men and women worked together in the fields, though at different tasks. Usually, the men used the foot plow while women sowed, broke down clods of earth, and used hoes for weeding. Women didn't work just for their households (or for their husbands) but for the *ayllu* as a whole. The labor unit was the whole household and included the women and even children once they were seven.

Cultivation of the land using a foot plow, with the women helping. Drawing by Guamán Poma de Ayala.

https://commons.wikimedia.org/wiki/File:Guam%C3%A1n_Poma_1615_1156_septiembre.png

The land was used in common by the *ayllu* but was distributed (and redistributed annually to take account of changes in demographics) according to the *tupu*, which was enough land to support a childless couple. The size of the *tupu* would be different depending on the type and fertility of the land.

Garcilaso de la Vega says the order of cultivation was firstly the fields of the sun, then the fields of anyone who was unable to work their own land, then everyone else's fields, then the fields of the *curacas*, and finally, the fields of the Sapa Inca. (However, not all chroniclers agree on this.) The priority given to the fields of those unable to work shows the typical Andean values of reciprocity and mutual support.

The *mink'a* method replaced collective work with a labor requirement. For instance, each household might have to devote one day a week to a particular communal project or task, such as herding the whole *ayllu's* livestock or maintaining or digging an irrigation channel. This helped distribute labor better since cultivation was distributed over a number of different zones in what has been called "vertical archipelagos."[6]

One of the major factors in making Inca agriculture productive was terracing. The Inca did not invent terracing; it had been used extensively by the Huari and other cultures, but they perfected it. For instance, the space between the walls was filled first with rough rocks, then gravel, then sand, and finally topsoil rather than only with soil. This had two big advantages. First, it strengthened the terraces and improved drainage, protecting the system against the possibility of soil slumping. Secondly, it economized on the amount of topsoil needed to be brought up from the valley bottom, often from dredging the river. There are now one million hectares of terraced land in the Andes, much of which was built by the Inca.

The stone walls didn't just hold back soil; they also heated up during the day and radiated that warmth at night, making it possible to grow plants above their normal altitude and reducing the likelihood of a single short freeze destroying the crops. The Inca didn't have glass, but the terraces fulfilled, in some ways, the same function as

---

[6] McEwan, Gordon F. *The Inca: New Perspectives*. ABC Clio, Santa Barbara, 2006. Pg. 84.

greenhouses.

Inca terraces at Moray.
JustinW on Pixabay. https://pixabay.com/photos/moray-peru-inca-landscape-290641/

Another improvement was the integration of terracing and irrigation. The Inca had huge expertise in waterworks, working out the exact gradient at which water needed to run to irrigate without scouring the soil and the right curves to take fast-running water where it needed to go. Many fields were supplied by aqueducts, and water drops were built into the terrace walls. In many cases, the water features are both functional and aesthetic.

Fields were fertilized by guano brought from the coastal regions, as well as by llama dung and dried fish heads.

The crops that were grown depended on the region and the height of the land. At high altitudes, root crops, such as potatoes, oca, and olluco, were the main crops. Quinoa, a kind of small grain, was cultivated up to four thousand meters.

On lower terraces, the "Three Sisters" (a term more commonly used in the US) of corn, beans, and squash could all be grown, and sweet potato and manioc were introduced from the eastern foothills. Yucca, tomatoes, peppers, and peanuts were also grown.

The Inca also had a huge variety of different types of each species. Different types of corn grew in different zones, and they had many different varieties of potato, which apparently were all bred from the original pea-sized plant. This enabled the Inca to take the best advantage of each location.

Yet the tools they employed were rudimentary. The foot plow was made of wood and sometimes had a bronze point or just a sharpened wooden point. It looked like a pogo stick with a point and a handle. Rather than digging furrows, it turned over a single clod of earth, which the women would break up. Fortunately, corn, potatoes, and other tubers can be sown into a simple hole and don't need to be put into furrows. Their hoes generally had a stone blade.

The Andes range is home to a number of different camelids. The Inca domesticated two: llamas and alpacas. Llamas were beasts of burden, while alpacas yielded wool for clothing. Vicuñas, which have the softest wool, were not domesticated, but they were rounded up every couple of years and shorn of their wool before being rereleased. Each household was allocated two llamas, which were not to be killed unless they were aging or ill.

At lower altitudes, cotton and non-food crops, such as gourds, which were used for storage, and various types of fiber for rope were grown.

Coca was grown in the eastern foothills. They came from the Amazon, so they were not technically part of the Inca Empire (forests were not their environment). However, the Inca held enough borderland to get products like exotic bird feathers and coca. It was usually chewed with lime; swallowing the resulting juice enabled its users to work long hours without tiring, and it could also provide pain relief.

Inca agriculture was remarkably productive, given the tough terrain. However, as the empire expanded, there was an argument that increasingly heavy tax demands led to the farming of marginal land. That came at a very high cost in terms of infrastructure investment and was less effective than existing cultivation. Dependence on marginal land made crop failures more likely and reduced returns, gradually impoverishing the empire.

Chapter 5: Inca Cuisine and Diet

What the subjects of the Inca Empire ate depended to some extent on where they lived. The highland diet was different from the marine-valley diet. On the coast, fish and shellfish were mixed with maize and other vegetables, while in the highlands, potatoes and other tubers were a staple. Quinoa and other related plants provided grains that could be used in ways similar to rice. Tomatoes, beans, and bell peppers were used in stews, and the Inca appear to have enjoyed spicing their food with chili peppers.

However, one thing that united most communities was that their diet was vegetarian or at least pescatarian most of the time. Only the nobility were allowed to hunt, and llamas were too useful in other ways for eating them to be a regular occurrence. (Strangely enough, the Inca did not drink llama milk, though it is quite palatable.) That left guinea pigs, which, over time, became domesticated and provided the main source of protein in the highlands. Frogs, ants, and other insects were also eaten.

Cooking methods included small, fuel-efficient clay stoves (*huatia*) and dropping hot rocks into water or stews to heat them up. Guinea pigs were often stuffed with hot rocks when they were cooked to ensure the flesh was evenly cooked inside and out.

The Inca did not have sugar and did not learn how to keep bees, but they knew how to find wild honey for sweetening.

But the element of Inca cuisine that was key to the success of the empire was simple: dehydrated food. Llama meat was dried in strips called charqui, which is where the word "jerky" comes from. Charqui made an excellent source of protein. It could be carried long distances and weighed very little. Potatoes were freeze-dried by being left out overnight to freeze, then trampled or ground to remove the skins; they were called chuño. Andean farmers still make chuño today. In the coastal areas, fish were air-dried.

Inca were able to store extensive supplies of non-perishable foodstuffs. Both the Tihuanaco and Huari cultures came to an end because of years of drought and famine; whether or not the Inca knew this, their decision to store food seems very sensible considering the problematic nature of the Peruvian climate. But storehouses along the roads also allowed the army to be supplied on campaigns, which must have greatly helped the logistics of extensive military campaigns.

Maize was used to make corn flour, cornbread, and cakes. The Inca were also quite partial to popcorn. However, maize was also important as the main ingredient in the alcoholic beverage chicha, known as *aqa* in Quechua. Chicha is a cloudy sweet beer that is still available in numerous chicherias in Cuzco and made by families and villages for feasts. The Inca did not drink water unless they were fasting; chicha was the most popular beverage.

The making of chicha was exclusively done by females. The *aclla* were taught to make chicha as part of their training, and during puberty rites, girls would make and serve beer as a reward for boys who completed their endurance ordeals. Chicha was poured in front of *huacas*, including mummies, and individuals would dip their fingers in chicha and flick it onto the earth as a small offering while drinking.

Feasting and drinking maintained power relationships among the nobility and also nourished the communal feeling among the people all over the empire. Most feasts probably ended with people overindulging, which is still the case in Quechua cultures today.

Contemporary cuisine in Peru and Bolivia uses ingredients that were introduced by the Spanish, such as rice, wheat, chicken, beef, and pork. But the main staples are still potatoes, corn, quinoa, and legumes. Olluquito con charqui is a traditional dish made with olluco (like a potato but crunchy). It is stewed with small pieces of charqui, but nowadays, it's usually served on rice instead of quinoa, and the charqui may be mutton rather than llama. Guinea pigs are still raised and eaten in many communities, and eating fried guinea pigs has become something of a ritual for backpackers visiting Peru.

Chapter 6: Arts and Science

Arts

The most well-known art of the Inca is their architecture, which is still visible in many places today, most notably in Cuzco and Machu Picchu. In many ways, their buildings were extremely simple but also highly refined in execution.

The two basic constructions are the *cancha* and the *callanca*. The *cancha* is a group of rectangular, single-story, single-room buildings around a courtyard, usually within a walled compound. Two-story buildings are often found where the slope of the ground on which the house is built allows both stories to have exits at the ground level.

The *callanca*, on the other hand, is a great hall with gabled ends and multiple doors on one side. *Callancas* normally form one side of a town's major plaza. They may have been temporary residences, or they may have been used for ceremonial purposes.

Thus, the Inca architectural plans are very simple. They lend themselves to grid-like townscapes. But they are frequently made in finely dressed stonework, as in Machu Picchu or in the walls of Coricancha. The masonry joints are made without mortar and are so tight that it is impossible to force a knife blade between the stones. Many of the stones are not rectangular but completely irregular. One of the most celebrated sights of Machu Picchu is the twelve-cornered stone that is neatly fitted among a dozen differently shaped smaller stones. The edges of the stones are often beveled, creating a fine chiaroscuro effect.

This masonry was created using only stone hammers and a few bronze tools, such as crowbars. Yet the rock that was used is not soft like limestone; it's generally hard igneous rock, such as andesite, diorite, or granite. The detailed fitting was not achieved with hand tools but by putting fine wet mud or sand between two stones and rubbing them together. This was highly labor intensive, but the use of sulfides from Inca mines could have helped to dissolve the silica-rich rock.[7]

Finely fitted stone walls in Cuzco.
Karloanson on Pixabay. https://pixabay.com/photos/stones-cusco-cuzco-city-of-cuzco-2608832/

A close look at some Inca masonry reveals a glazed and polished appearance of the rock close to the joints as if it had been vitrified. That bears out the suggestion that chemical reactions played a part in the process. In the highest quality work, for instance, in Machu Picchu's sacred plaza, the fit is exact inside and out. In other works, while the exterior is perfectly finished, the inside wall is less well made, with cracks filled by smaller stones. This would almost certainly have been plastered.

Much of the stonework features stone "nubbins" or bosses, which may have been chiseled off at completion in most cases.

[7] Tributsch, Helmut. "On The Reddish, Glittery Mud the Inca Used for Perfecting Their Stone Masonry." SDRP Journal of Earth Sciences & Environmental Studies 3 (1), 309-323. 2018.

A key feature of Inca buildings is the batter or taper of around five or six degrees from the vertical. This is seen not only in the walls but also in doors, windows, and niches. In an earthquake-prone zone, the batter would add strength to the walls, but it also has a clear aesthetic appeal. Doorways are trapezoidal and often have double or even triple jambs as an accent in high-class buildings.

Windows are very rarely found, so buildings would have been lit through the doors. Niches are found both internally and externally; some were used as cupboards, while others may have held mummies, idols, or other *huacas*. The Inca did not have furniture. Stone platforms and stone pegs in the wall for hanging bags have been found. Those of the highest rank could use low-carved stools, but this may have only been for use in ceremonies.

What remains of Inca architecture is bare walls. Some imagination is required to reconstruct the appearance of the buildings with their steeply pitched, thatched roofs. At Machu Picchu, Hiram Bingham discovered protruding cylindrical roof pegs and "eye-bonders" around which rope would have secured the various grasses used for the thatch.

A view of Machu Picchu.
Patburdubc0 on Pixabay. <u>*https://pixabay.com/photos/machu-pichu-peru-ruins-inca-540145/*</u>

In many cases, the buildings would have had their interior and sometimes exterior walls covered by brightly colored plaster. Some of Huayna Capac's buildings at his Quispiguanca estate preserved traces of rich orange and red paint, while another palace in Yucay shows bright green, red, turquoise, and white paint in the niches that decorate its façade.

Outcrops of natural stone are often incorporated into buildings. This must have been practical, but it is also likely that it had a religious aspect. In a royal estate, the outcrops would tie the Sapa Inca to the supernatural power of the mountain *huaca*. There were also viewing platforms to see mountains, which were also connected with the *huacas* and the sense of a sacred landscape.

Building was a way of giving form to history. The Sapa Incas were expected to build. As soon as the former Sapa Inca was dead, the Inca began building a palace for the new Sapa Inca. To some extent, the new Sapa Inca began the work of becoming an ancestor, providing palaces and estates for his *panaca* to enable his mummy to be adequately looked after.

However, the real genius of the Inca and the second largest sector of the economy behind agriculture was textile creation. There were three grades of cloth: blanket cloth, general clothing textiles, and fine cumbi cloth, which was worn only by the nobles and was also used as a burnt offering to the gods. One hundred cumbi cloths were burned every morning in Cuzco to the rising sun. Cumbi cloth was also often given to nobles and officials as a reward and to conquered peoples as a gift for joining the Inca Empire.

This cloth was considered more valuable than gold. The cloth was never cut, so all clothes were based on simple woven rectangles. Women wore a cloth wrap with a mantle pinned over their shoulders, while men wore a tunic over a loincloth. The *tupu* (clothespin) was used by women to keep their clothes in place. These pins had huge elliptical heads and have been frequently found as artifacts. They were made of various metals (nobles wore gold, while the lower classes generally used copper or bronze). Cotton and alpaca wool were both used and woven on either backstrap looms (where the weaver tied the warp threads to a tree or post and the other end of the thread around their back) or upright looms.

Topa Inca's tunic, which was woven from cotton and vicuña wool.
https://commons.wikimedia.org/wiki/File:Tupa-inca-tunic.png

Brightly patterned and colored designs reflected status and group membership. The patterns might have particular meanings. Red, yellow, and orange were often the predominant colors. Blue, on the other hand, is rarely found. Red was associated with conquest and blood, black with creation and death, and yellow with maize or gold. Feathers were particularly prized and woven into fabric and used for headdresses.

However, the patterns were repetitive, with only a small number of different decorative elements, such as squares and feather patterns. Even jaguars, pumas, and snakes were shown as geometric abstractions. Guamán Poma's pictures show clothing with small squares in a regular grid pattern filled with ornaments, such as checker patterns. Unfortunately, these are only line drawings, so you have to imagine the bright colors for yourself.

Guamán Poma de Ayala's drawing of Tupac Yupanqui wearing a finely woven tunic.
https://commons.wikimedia.org/wiki/File:Tupac_Yupanqui_por_Guaman_Poma_de_Ayala.jpg

Basic spinning and weaving would have been done in every *ayllu* as a part of providing for the needs of the community. Expert weavers were frequently taken to Cuzco; the women in the *acllahuasi* also wove high-quality fabrics. Similar textiles are made today but not to the same degree of quality as the Inca achieved.

Just as textiles were standardized, so were ceramics. This standardization emphasized Inca superiority over subject peoples and, like the textiles, involved the use of repetitive, geometrical patterns.

The human figure was hardly ever used as a subject; where it is seen, it is fully clothed. The cold of the Andes explains that, but it was also considered taboo. That's a big contrast with the Moche culture, which joyfully celebrated the everyday life of its people in its ceramics.

Since the Inca didn't have the potter's wheel, they molded their pottery in two parts and then joined them together with a slip. The work is very fine and was fired at high temperatures, creating hard, polished red or buff pottery.

The Inca were also fine metallurgists, working gold, silver, copper, and bronze. Gold was found in streams by panning and was sometimes trench mined. The nobility had a monopoly on the use of precious metals, so commoners used copper or bronze for ornaments. Bronze was also used for some tools. Gold was not used as a currency or means of exchange; it was purely decorative. Coricancha's walls were sheathed with gold, and the Sapa Inca was said to have a garden with gold and silver flowers and even animals in it. Gold llama and Inca figures have been found buried at holy sites.

Gold was cold hammered, embossed, repousséd, soldered, and cast in both open and closed molds—quite an extensive repertoire of techniques.

Unfortunately, much of the Inca art was transitory. We don't know what their music was like, though they played flutes similar to those played by Andean musicians today, such as end-blown flutes and panpipes. Conch shells were used as trumpets. Bells, rattles, and drums were used in rhythm sections, but stringed instruments were not known.

Just a few specimens of Inca poetry have been preserved by early chroniclers. Juan de Betanzos, who married a Sapa Inca's concubine, learned to speak Quechua and preserved a praise song, which was one of the ways the Inca maintained their history. It is notable for its extensive use of internal rhyme, which must have made it easier to remember and given it an incredible musicality.

"Ynga Yupangue yndin
Yocafola ymalca
Chinboleifolaymalca
Axcoley Haguaya guaya
Haguaya guaya."

"Inca Yupanqui, son of the Sun, conquered the Soras and made them wear fringes."[8] The fringes were put on the garments of subject peoples as a sign of their subordinate status.

Garcilaso de la Vega, who was half-Inca, quoted a simple love poem in his chronicle:

"In this place

Thou shalt sleep

Midnight

I will come."[9]

And Pachacuti's deathbed poem has been preserved in two different versions. As he was dying, he uttered these melancholy words:

"I was born as a flower of the field,

As a flower I was cherished in my youth,

I came to my full age, I grew old,

Now I am withered and die."[10]

Science

The Inca had a good understanding of mathematics and a standardized measuring system. They used decimals in their administration and understood the concept of zero, which had its own place on the quipu.

The use of the quipu for recording has already been mentioned. It appears to have been considerably more than a mere counting device. However, for calculations, it was useless; counting boards that were cut in stone were used instead, with pebbles that could be moved from one compartment to another.

This would not have allowed the Inca to do the kind of complex calculations that the contemporary Maya could carry out, but it allowed basic multiplication and addition. Depending on where a

---

[8] Niles, Susan A. *The Shape of Inca History: Narrative and Architecture in an Andean Empire.* University of Iowa Press, 1999. Pg. 29.

[9] Malpass, Michael A. *Daily Life in the Inca Empire.* Greenwood Press, Westport, CT, 1996. Pg. 89.

[10] McEwan, Gordon F. *The Inca: New Perspectives.* Pg. 182.

---

pebble was put on the board, its value would be multiplied by two, three, six, or twelve. Different colored pebbles could represent different objects, allowing calculations for different things to be carried out at the same time (e.g., different age groups in a village).

The Inca appear to have been quite pragmatic mathematicians. They were not interested in advanced calculation or theory, and in the same way, their astronomical knowledge was directed toward pragmatic ends, such as knowing when to plant and when to harvest. The Maya were far more advanced, partly because they considered certain numbers to be sacred. They used base twenty and had mathematical symbols that allowed addition and subtraction to be carried out easily.

The Maya also used their mathematics for detailed astronomical calculations that allowed them to create a perpetual calendar; this actually had a slight edge over the calendar being used in Europe at the time.

The Inca were not ignorant of how to use astronomy for the purposes they considered important. For instance, they built towers in the cardinal directions around Cuzco so that when they were viewed from the *ushna* (the dais in the main square), they could clearly indicate the dates for equinoxes and solstices, from which planting and harvest dates could be calculated.

The Inca also ran two separate calendars simultaneously. The daytime calendar was based on solar observations and had 365 solar days, while the lunar (night) calendar of 328 days was used to find the correct dates for ceremonies devoted to the moon and stars. The use of two calendars may reflect the Incas' organization of society and religion into complementary pairings of the moon and the sun, male and female, Sapa Inca and coya, and earth and water.

Pachacuti is said to have standardized the ritual calendar, which had ceremonies for each month. According to Brundage, "His interest was less in the perfecting of abstruse time calculations and stellar observations than in the dramatization of the spiritual life of his people."[11] The ceremonies were created for the purpose of bringing the people together in submission to the gods, in particular Inti, and

---

[11] Brundage, Burr Cartwright. *Empire of the Inca.* Pg. 171.

were not related to an overarching cosmological view, such as what the Maya possessed.

Things the Inca Did Not Have
• the wheel
• screws
• iron
• furniture
• files
• scissors
• glue
• the potter"s wheel
• compasses
• T- squares
• tongs
• bellows
• saws
• bows and arrows (except for troops from Antisuyu)
• drill bits
• currency
• writing

The Inca practiced herbal medicine and used a large number of different herbs and plants in their remedies. However, they believed that spirits were always involved in the process of disease and healing. Sickness came from an imbalance of some kind, which could be corrected by appealing to a *huaca* or making a sacrifice.

Some surgical techniques were used; there is evidence of trepanning (cutting holes in the skull), and many of the skulls show evidence of bone regrowth. It's possible that 90 percent of patients survived. However, whether the treatment did any good is not known, though it may have been practiced as a means of relieving pressure on the skull from a war injury, in which case it may have been effective.

Coca was probably used as an anesthetic.

There is also some evidence of gold dental fillings, though these may have been intended more for aesthetic than health reasons.

The weaponry available to the Inca was basic but highly effective. Projectiles included the slingshot, which was highly accurate. Boys would have practiced shooting at birds in the fields from an early age. Spears with throwing sticks were also used. The army usually started a fight with projectile weapons before moving on to personal weapons, such as clubs and maces. These were sometimes made of bronze but were more often made of stone and wood. Bows and arrows were only used by the subject peoples from Amazonian areas in the east of the empire. Swords also appear not to have been known.

Another weapon used to great effect by the Inca was the bolas, which were stone balls at the end of leather thongs that were thrown. They would wrap around the feet of an enemy. These were also used for hunting by the Inca nobility.

Chapter 7: Demographics and Religion

Demographics

It is quite difficult to estimate the population of the Inca Empire at the time of the Spanish invasion. Atahualpa destroyed many of the empire's records, and the Spanish destroyed more. Most of the quipus that survived came from tombs, and it is unlikely that census records were provided as grave goods. Besides, we still don't know exactly how to read them.

Estimates vary greatly, ranging from between 6 million and 37.5 million. Different techniques have been used to estimate how many people might have inhabited the empire. For instance, it has been estimated that the land, as cultivated by the Inca, could have supported around thirteen million people.

Another way of working out the figures is to take the population after the Spanish conquest and adjust for the depopulation that occurred. In 1946, an archaeologist and anthropologist named John Howland Rowe used figures from provinces where the population was known after the conquest. He assumed a depopulation rate of 4:1 and came up with six million. Another researcher used a 25:1 depopulation ratio and came up with an original population of 37.5 million, but this is very much an outlier. Besides, it is debatable whether the land could have supported such a high population.

It seems likely that the population of the empire was somewhere between six and twelve million. We know that by 1580, it was no more than eight million.

However, this refers to the population of the Inca Empire. Of these, only around forty thousand were Inca, with the remainder being made up of subject peoples. The Inca were vastly in the minority. Their concern with lineage and purity of blood meant that though the empire was unified by language and by broad cultural assimilation, the Inca people remained separate from the bulk of the population.

From the time of Pachacuti onward, Quechua was the language of the empire. The sons of *curacas* were educated in Quechua so that by the next generation, the ruler of any new conquest would be a Quechua speaker and able to work in the official language. However, the languages of other people varied. Aymara was and still is spoken in the former Tiahuanaco lands, and there were variants of Quechua, such as Puquina in the south and Mochica on the northern coasts. Quingnam, Mapudungun, Chachapoya, Jaqaru, and Barbacoan languages, among others, were also spoken in different parts of the empire. Today, there are forty-five different variants of Quechua; Quechua and Aymara remain the two major languages of the region.

The *ayllu*, or clan, was the primary social organization. Marriages were usually endogenous, that is, within the *ayllu*, and both labor and ritual activities brought the *ayllu* together. The *ayllu* owned and cultivated its own land in most Andean cultures. However, the Inca "nationalized" land through the theory that the Sapa Inca owned it, making the *ayllu* into a unit of tax administration; in other words, they adapted an existing social organization to the needs of the empire.

Marriage in the Inca Empire was compulsory. If a man reached twenty-five without being married, the *curaca* would choose a wife for him. The usual age of marriage for a woman was sixteen, but she could get married as late as twenty. The *aclla* were the only exception to this rule.

Marriage within the *ayllu* was presumably arranged between the parents or partners, but marriages might have also been arranged by simply lining up those of marriageable age and having the men choose a wife, although the *curaca* also might have decided. A marriage appears to have been seen as a practical and reciprocal relationship (both bride and bridegroom exchanged gifts), and marriage entitled a man to be treated as an adult.

Except for the Inca nobility, monogamy was the rule. Even within the nobility, one wife was always the principal wife. A secondary wife could never become a principal wife, even if the principal wife died. The Inca nobility would often have their marriage partners chosen by the Sapa Inca or, in the case of women, by the coya. The Sapa Inca had less choice than anyone since he had to choose one of his full-blood sisters.

Adultery was punishable by death. However, premarital sex was common and raised no eyebrows, something Catholic priests still have to turn a blind eye to in many Quechua villages.

The dead were part of the *ayllu* and part of the family. They were often buried in *chullpas*, funerary chambers like small towers or houses available to the entire *ayllu*. The Mexican Day of the Dead is well known today, but the Inca and other Andean peoples also had a November festival where their ancestors would be visited and given a feast. Stories of the ancestors of the *ayllu* were probably told as well.

Gender roles within Andean societies were seen as complementary. Women had their own lineage and their own rites. While women and men had different tasks in the fields, they worked together and cooperated. There is evidence that suggests women may have held power or exercised it jointly with their husbands, though the increased class differentiation of the Inca Empire appears to have included a decrease in women's power. Even so, several coyas are remembered as being particularly influential. Pachacuti's coya, Mama Ocllo, suggested a stratagem to take a city in Chimor that was ruled by a woman. (It may have been considered suitable for a woman, rather than the Sapa Inca, to accept the submission of another woman.)

The Inca never picked up babies, as it was considered such a move would make them "soft." To breastfeed, the mother would bend over the child, which was expected to latch on, just like a baby llama. Work for most (except the nobility) started early. A seven-year-old child would work, though it would be easy work at first. Boys would shoot and scare birds away from the crops, which was useful and also taught them skills for later military service.

Boys continued to toughen up with their puberty rituals, which included a number of ordeals, including vigils, whipping, fasting, and mountain ascents. They were given gifts by their family, but when they acted out, they were whipped on the legs to stop them from being too soft.

There was no freedom of movement. Most people stayed in their own villages unless they were required to work elsewhere, such as in the army or on a major project, such as road building. Anyone on the road would have official business. Since subjects were required to wear their traditional clothes and headgear, it would be known if they were attempting to move without permission. If they went to Cuzco, as *curacas* might do, they had to lodge in the quarter of the city that corresponded to their province's place in the empire.

Education was only for the ruling classes and the "chosen women." Boys learned Quechua, the Inca religion, the use of the quipu, and Inca history for four years in Cuzco. They were taught by the *amautas* (teachers). The *aclla* might learn in Cuzco or in a provincial house of women. Spinning, weaving, cooking, religion, and the making of chicha made up their four-year course.

Religion

The Inca religion was derived from common Andean traditions, which saw the world as being made up of duality that needed to be held in balance. Gods might have different names in different places and have slightly different concerns, but there were three main deities: a creator god, who was fairly distant (in Inca mythology, Viracocha wandered off into the Pacific after observing his creation); a mother goddess who was linked to the moon and water; and a god of the weather and mountains.

A 1615 drawing of the cosmic model that was displayed in Coricancha shows the oppositions of the sky and earth, the sun and moon, the morning and evening star, and summer and winter. Male and female was another key duality. In the Inca religion, there is a male "chain" that links Inti, the sun, the morning star, the Inca, and all men. There was also a female "chain" linking Mama Quilla, the moon, the evening star, the coya, and all women. On Lake Titicaca, the god and goddess each have an island in the middle of the lake. This balance runs all the way through the Inca religion. Only Viracocha, who was shown as an egg or an oval, transcends duality; he is the origin, the balance, and contains male and female and all other dualities within himself.

Viracocha created the world. He brought the sun and moon out of Lake Titicaca, formed men and animals, and painted each tribe's clothing, showing that the differentiation observed by the Inca between the different peoples went back to the creator. Viracocha then traveled north. He reached Ecuador and walked out to sea, but he might someday return. The idea of his return would play an interesting role when the Spanish arrived. The lack of resistance on the part of some Inca may have been because of their belief that Francisco Pizarro was the returning Viracocha.

According to historians Geoffrey Conrad and Arthur Demarest, "The most convincing generalizations about Mesoamerican religion view the pantheon as a personification of specific segments or nodes in the sacred cosmic order, and continuum of time and space itself."[12] That is, the underlying beliefs in order and balance did not vary, though individual gods might differ. Since the "divine complex" was multi-faceted, any god could take individual aspects while not denying any of the others.

This was one of the reasons the Inca Empire flourished. The Inca did not see any reason why subject peoples should not continue to worship their own gods (as long as they paid their taxes) since these gods did not pose any competition to Inti and the other Inca gods. However, the Inca did sometimes take idols hostage. They took them to Cuzco to ensure a newly conquered people's good behavior. After the Spanish conquest, the Inca adapted the Virgin Mary to the Andean goddess Pachamama. The Virgin Mary's cult in Bolivia and Peru has very strong reminiscences of Pachamama (for instance, she is given libations of chicha), and in many cases, a church dedicated to her took over a Pachamama shrine.

The Inca origin myth shows the male/female balance overtly. Mama Huaco, as Manco Cápac's sister-wife, is equated with Pachamama, the most common Andean female deity. This balance was reflected in many rituals. For instance, the marriage of the Sapa Inca to his sister-wife formed part of the coronation rituals, and both partners were exalted in the rites. The ceremonial dance toward Coricancha at great festivals saw women dancing on one side and men

---

[12] Conrad, Geoffrey & Demarest, Arthur A. *Religion and Empire: The Dynamics of Aztec and Inca Expansionism.* Pg. 18.

on the other. And even in colonial times, some villages had two idols: one male idol owned by a man who inherited it from his father and a female idol that was passed down the female line. However, over time, as the Inca grew from a tribe to an imperialist power, the solar deity Inti came to dominate the Inca pantheon.

Inti was the one deity who was exclusively worshiped by the Inca. He was the sun disc, a conqueror, and the father of the Inca clans and of the Sapa Inca himself. When great celebrations of the Inti cult were being held, non-Inca and non-native *huacas* (such as idols brought from other temples) were expelled from the inner city of Cuzco. A prayer to Inti that has survived shows how closely Inti was integrated into the empire's ideology of conquest:

"O Sun, my father, who said 'let there be Cuzco!' and by your will it was founded and it is preserved with such grandeur! Let these sons of yours, the Inca, be conquerors and despoilers of all mankind. We adore you and offer this sacrifice to you so that you will grant us what we beg of you. Let them be prosperous and make them happy, and do not allow them to be conquered by anyone, but let them always be conquerors since you made them for that purpose."[13]

Originally, Illapa, the god of the sky, thunder, and rain, was the male counterpart to Pachamama, the generic Andean mother goddess. However, the Inca replaced these generic Andean gods with Inti and Mama Quilla, the sun and the moon. (When people worshiped Inti, they were also worshiping their ruler, the Sapa Inca; religious and political ideologies were unified.) Illapa remained in the pantheon but was reduced in status.

Andean peoples also believed that certain places in the landscape were sacred, such as springs, caves, and mountains, which the Inca called *huacas*, along with other sacred things, such as the mummies of ancestors and sites of major battles and other events. Here again, the Inca religion does not differ from the existing religions of most peoples in the region.

When the Inca took over some well-known sacred sites, they integrated them into their pantheon. For instance, the oracle shrine of Pachacamac, near Lima, predated the Inca, having been built in

---

[13] McEwan, Gordon F. *The Inca: New Perspectives*. Pg. 181.

around 600 CE as part of the Huari cult. The Inca coopted this creator god, although they considered him inferior to Viracocha, and added an *acllahuasi* to the complex.

The birth house and death house of a Sapa Inca would become *huacas*, and the point at which a traveler topped the pass into the valley and first saw Cuzco was a *huaca* too. Even an amulet might be a *huaca*. Rock outcrops were often carved into "sun hitching posts" (*intihuatana*), and the rocks surrounding springs might also be carved. It is possible that the finely structured fountains of some of the royal estates had a sacred meaning, as well as being the origin of the irrigation canals for the estate.

The Andean religions also emphasized the idea that the dead were still active in the world, though in a different manner from the living. Ancestor worship did not begin with the Inca; for instance, the museum in Trujillo, Peru, contains a clay model from the Chimú culture that shows a shrine in which a mummy is being venerated. Food would be brought to the house in which bodies were placed, and the dead were always consulted before making decisions.

Despite this, the Inca also seem to have had a concept of an afterlife, which, like the Inca society, was class differentiated; the nobility would go to *hanan pacha*, the world above, while common people went to *ukhu pacha*, the world below.

We have an example of a prayer to the ancestors:

"O fathers, guacas, and vilcas, our grandfathers and ancestors! Protect these little children of yours so that they will be happy and very fortunate as you are yourself; intercede with Viracocha on their behalf; bring them closer to him so he will give them the protection that he gives to you."[14]

---

[14]McEwan, Gordon F. *The Inca: New Perspectives*. Pg. 181.

Inca Gods

Viracocha	Creator god, now absent
Inti	Sun god, specifically the god of the Inca conquest and the father of the Sapa Inca
Mama Quilla	Moon goddess (an aspect of Pachamama), the female counterpart of Inti
Illapa	Weather/rain/thunder god; in earlier Andean religion, the male counterpart of Mamacocha; superseded in the Inca pantheon by Inti
Supay	Underworld god (translated inaccurately as "devil" by the Spanish)
Pachamama	Mother goddess, worshiped under various aspects ("daughters")
Mamacocha	Sea mother or water mother
Mamasara	Mother of corn—a specific aspect of Mamacocha
And also worshiped:	
Mallqui	Mummies/ancestors
Huaca	Sacred places

The Inca created a huge religious establishment that had a great deal of formality and ritual. The priest of Inti was always a relative of the Sapa Inca (he was often his brother). He headed a large priesthood, including *mamaconas* (priestesses) from the chosen women. Temples were primarily seen as houses for the deity and ancestors. Communal worship happened in the main square of

Cuzco. The deities and mummies of the Sapa Incas and coyas would be brought out of the temple and seated in the place of honor. All ceremonies ended with a feast and the drinking of chicha. Dancing was often involved, but it was slow and ceremonial in nature; the Inca did not appear to have had a concept of dancing for fun.

Sacrifice was a major part of the Inca religion. Often, it might involve simply laying coca leaves in front of a *huaca*, pouring out chicha on the ground, or leaving food. Another frequent form of sacrifice was the burning of cumbi cloth. At some shrines, seashells, a symbol of water, were smashed and then buried.

Guinea pigs might be sacrificed, but the most common blood sacrifice was that of a llama. Brown llamas were sacrificed to Viracocha, white llamas to Inti, and mixed-colored llamas to Illapa. Idols and mummies would be smeared with their blood; mummies usually had blood smeared across their faces or masks.

Human sacrifice was also practiced but on a much smaller scale than in Central American societies, particularly the Aztec Empire. Human sacrifice was generally reserved for two events: coronations and wars. Prisoners of war might be sacrificed, though generally if a tribe submitted to Inca rule, this would not be done. Otherwise, the victims were usually children aged ten to fifteen, and they were always non-Inca. They feasted and drank coca or chicha, after which they were strangled, buried alive, or bludgeoned. Sometimes, their throats were cut. It is not known for certain why these children were targeted for sacrifices.

At times, child sacrifices were sent out from Cuzco to *huacas* in faraway provinces. The freeze-dried bodies of children sacrificed to mountains are only now being discovered on top of mountains like Llullaillaco and Aconcagua. These "Inca mummies" are not related to the mummy bundles of the Sapa Incas and ancestors; the mummification in the case of the child sacrifices was accidental. However, the incredible state of the remains has given archaeologists a huge amount of information, including examples of Inca textiles.

Various types of divination were practiced. For instance, someone might chew coca and then spit the juice into their hand, observing the patterns that it formed, or they might throw pebbles. Burning coca or llama fat could also be used to create smoke that would make patterns in the air. Another type of divination was associated with sacrifices and involved blowing up a lung from a slaughtered animal like a balloon and then observing the patterns on the inflated membrane.

Some major shrines had their own oracles. The Apurímac River had its own oracle, a post with two golden breasts attached to it (this was perhaps a way to attach human characteristics to the river). The name Apurímac means "Great Speaker." There was also an oracle at Pachacamac on the coast.

Rites, such as puberty rites, were not individual but collective rites. In Cuzco, puberty rites were held annually in the month of Capac Raymi (December) for all boys who qualified for them. The rite included a series of ordeals:

- It began with a period of fasting.
- The boys were sent to gather tough grass to make their own sandals.
- They climbed the sacred mountain Huanacauri and kept vigil.
- They were violently whipped at several stages during the rites.
- They had their ears pierced and were given the ear plugs that distinguished the pure-blooded Inca.
- They assembled in the main square in front of the Sapa Incas (past and present), where the deeds of the Inca were recited.
- They had to race down the steep sides of Mount Anahuarque, at the bottom of which the girls whose puberty had been celebrated that year waited with huge jars of chicha.
- At the end of the rites, they received their adult names and participated in the city-wide ceremonies at the end of the month.

Some of this ritual sounds like the worst kind of "ragging," something that a young man at a British Empire boarding school would have to endure. Both the reasoning and the imperialistic atmosphere were probably fairly similar.

Marriages were also a collective rite for the Inca, at least in many cases. At the most important stages in their lives, the Inca were bound into the collective, and as they became full members of their tribe, they recognized the power of their emperor and his lineage. Since the Inca had no writing, some call them prehistoric, but they were very aware of their own history, which was repeated at every ceremony.

PART THREE: EXPANSION AND THE SPANISH CONQUEST

Chapter 8: Expansion to the North

So far, the Inca ruled only the area immediately around Cuzco and the Yucay Valley. Pachacuti created an imperial ideology and bureaucracy, but it was his son, Topa Inca Yupanqui, who, first as a war leader and then as the Sapa Inca, expanded the empire toward the north and as far as the coast.

Topa Inca Yupanqui was born about 1448, ten years after his father's accession. He was made co-ruler at the age of sixteen and married Mama Ocllo, his sister, the year after the raid on Cajamarca.

The Chimú people and their realm of Chimor on the coast had been aware of the rise of the Inca. But the Inca were not close. Their rise had not threatened them. But the move by Pachacuti's brother, Cápac Inca Yupanqui, on Cajamarca brought the Inca to the notice of Chimor. The fracture lines were becoming apparent.

During the co-regency, from about 1463 to 1470, the Inca were taken up with the pacification of the empire's northern quarter. Topa Inca was sent north with ten thousand men and three generals, with the latter being close family. At first, he did not need to fight. He simply pitched his camp in full view of the Huancas of Jauja and waited. When the *sinchi* of Jauja turned up, he was given fine gifts and hospitality, then sent back to his tribe. This display, together with Topa Inca's diplomacy, must have explained the benefits of belonging to a wealthy and expanding polity, inducing the Huancas to join voluntarily as subjects of the Inca Empire.

Topa Inca arrived in Cajamarca, which was already held by the empire, and fortified it more strongly. He also brought in Inca to settle as a part of *mitma*, thus ensuring a firm Inca presence. This would have given him a good flow of information on any unrest from the natives and spread Inca culture more widely. The Inca could now push up into Ecuador and even as far as the southern part of Colombia. Chimor was next on the list.

Chimor had been founded around 900 CE on the northern coast of Peru, so it was a more mature society than the Inca. Its expansion began at about the same time as the Inca, around 1200 CE. Its institutions appear to have been similar to the Inca; the rulers claimed divine descent, and ancestor worship and split inheritance were practiced (so the dead rulers' property was administered by their estate and did not descend to the next ruler).

The capital at Chan Chan had an urban center of six square kilometers, although it was situated within a much larger area of less dense settlement. It was built mainly of adobe. The arid atmosphere of the coastal desert has allowed it to survive in good condition, and the ruins have been extensively excavated.

The city included ten large sequentially built palaces or citadels in the middle of the city, which included large burial platforms and the bodies of sacrificed women. These citadels were not sealed, so it is possible that bodies were brought into the main plazas for processions in certain ceremonies. The distribution and nature of the dwellings in Chan Chan show that, like the Inca, the Chimú had a class-differentiated social system. However, they appear to have worshiped the moon, considering it more powerful than the solar deity.

Inheritors of the Moche traditions, the Chimú had a much more varied and naturalistic approach to ceramics and art. Also, unlike the straitlaced Inca, they had no problem with human sexuality (something profusely illustrated in the pottery of their predecessors, the Moche). However, like the Inca, they were expansionist; having started in the Moche Valley, they expanded all the way along the coast to the north and south.

Minchancaman, the Chimú Capac, continued this expansion and took Huarmey, Chimor's southernmost territory on the coast. He then concentrated on the kingdom of Cuismancu, which lay between

Chimú and Inca territory. So, the early 1460s set the stage for the showdown between the Inca and the Chimú. Topa Inca advanced into Chimor and managed to loot several towns, but he could not sustain his campaign. So, he moved farther north.

First, he subdued the Cañari and took their capital of Tomebamba (now Cuenca, Ecuador). This was a major victory. Topa Inca resettled many of the Cañari farther south, sending a number to Cuzco. These massive deportations ensured the territory could be properly settled. The Inca administration started work on the Royal Road through the area and removed the threat of a rebellion behind the front lines. After two years of campaigning, Topa Inca returned to Cuzco to celebrate his triumph.

He was soon back to war, this time heading to Quito from his secure base of Tomebamba. If his labor program had made progress on building the Royal Road as far as Tomebamba, that would have greatly helped with the logistics of the campaign. It was a hard war, but the Inca finally ground down their opponents. Topa Inca was now based in the north. His heir, Huayna Capac, was born in Tomebamba (hence the name of his *panaca*, Tomebamba panaca), not in Cuzco.

But the coast, not Quito, was the ultimate goal. Having taken the north, Topa Inca could now use a pincer movement to outflank Chimor. He headed toward Tumbez on the coast to the west of Quito and took the city. (Ironically, it was Tumbez where Pizarro and his Spanish expedition first arrived by boat.) Having taken Tumbez, Topa Inca then sent half his army south under Auqui Yupanqui and Tillca Yupanqui while the other part of the army pushed up the coast from the south. Chan Chan was now caught between the two parts of the Inca army, and its ruler, Minchancaman, had no option but to submit. This likely happened around 1470, a year before Topa Inca's accession as the Sapa Inca.

Minchancaman was taken to Cuzco, and his son was made ruler in his place, serving as an Inca puppet. Minchancaman married one of Topa Inca's daughters, tying the ruling family of Chimor firmly into the Inca establishment. However, Chimor was not completely conquered with the taking of Chan Chan; efforts to complete the conquest continued well into the 1470s.

The victory was a remarkable testimony to the strategic thinking of Topa Inca. But the most remarkable thing about this victory was that the Inca army was fighting at sea level and in the heat of the desert. Typically, most of the troops lived and trained at eleven thousand feet.

Topa Inca once more headed to Cuzco to celebrate. This time, after the victory celebrations, he took full control of the empire. Pachacuti may have abdicated, or he may have been pushed out by a coup d'état similar to the one he had organized against Viracocha.

Topa Inca next concentrated on the area of the coast south of Cuismancu. This was a less rich land than Chimor but still held numerous fertile oases, including the site of today's capital of Peru, Lima. The people of this region also traded as far inland as Lake Titicaca. Topa Inca took advantage of his campaign to visit the renowned temple of Pachacamac, where he questioned the oracle. He carefully absorbed the god Pachacamac into the Inca religion, though he made the god subservient to Viracocha. He also created roads between the Lima area and Cuzco and moved Inca and other subject peoples into the region to ensure the subservience of the people.

However, the Huarca people were hard to subdue. Topa Inca took a remarkable step to subdue them; he built a city known as Incahuasi. It was a garrison town in the canyon near Huarco. According to John Hyslop, Incahuasi was a "New Cuzco," a symbolic facsimile of the Inca capital surrounded by *ceque* lines connecting sacred sites, just like Cuzco. The new city consisted of four square miles. It took Topa Inca four years to besiege the Huarca. Once it was taken, he had the defenders slaughtered and transformed the adobe fort into a stone-walled Inca stronghold. New Cuzco was abandoned; it had done its job.

After this, Topa Inca expanded the empire up the coast and into Ecuador, but the job was not complete, as the new territories had not been completely consolidated. When Huayna Capac succeeded him as the Sapa Inca, there was a general uprising in the north. The new Sapa Inca's reign would be devoted to consolidating the north of the empire. This was intended to strengthen the empire, but it actually weakened it considerably and indirectly led to the civil war that stopped the Inca from defending themselves effectively against the Spanish.

Fortunately, the southern part of the empire was at peace. This enabled Huayna Capac to concentrate on the northern provinces. It also allowed him to call on the south for men and supplies. Since he took the best warriors of the Lupaca and Colla peoples on his campaign, he also deprived the south of all the leaders of a potential rebellion.

Twenty-three-year-old Huayna Capac left his young son, Huáscar, in Cuzco, in the charge of Huaman Achachi as regent; he put his elder brother, Auqui Topa Inca, and someone named Michi in charge of the army. Huayna Capac settled in Tomebamba. At first, Tomebamba was probably just a northern center of operations, but it seems to have gradually become a northern capital.

The Caranqui of northern Ecuador had cut off the northern Inca garrisons and were beginning to menace Quito. When Huayna Capac set out against them, he was overwhelmingly defeated. He needed to call new Inca troops from Cuzco. And at this point, he made a tactical mistake: he decided to humiliate the leaders who had failed him in the assault on the Caranqui.

In response, Michi led a mutiny of the Inca against the Sapa Inca. He stole the army's *huaca* (an idol representing the mountain god Huanacauri) from the temple and started to march back to Cuzco.

Huayna Capac was able to pay him off with treasure and women from the *acllahuasi*, but this must have dramatically damaged the Sapa Inca's prestige. The army now knew that he could be blackmailed.

Brundage speculates that the empire had grown to a size where Huayna Capac may have realized that government officials of only pure Inca blood could no longer work. He was working toward ending the Inca monopoly, which set him on a collision course with his top military advisors. Certainly, the empire was becoming overwhelmingly large, and the distance between Tomebamba and Cuzco, in particular, presented major difficulties in administering the empire efficiently.

Auqui Toma, the brother of the Sapa Inca, was chosen to lead a second assault on the Caranqui and nearly succeeded but was killed before the fortress could be taken. Huayna Capac took command of the third assault on the Caranqui. This time, he used clever tactics rather than force. After dividing his army into three divisions, he moved two of them to support Inca-held forts elsewhere. However, as soon as they were out of sight, these divisions doubled back and were held in reserve near the battlefield.

Huayna Capac attacked the Caranqui fortress. He spent some time in battle before sounding the retreat. The Caranqui came out fighting, sure they had the upper hand against the relatively small number Huayna Capac had under his command. They were determined to slaughter and loot the fleeing Inca.

At this moment, the two other divisions of the Inca army came out of hiding and attacked the Caranqui from both sides. What happened next must have been similar to *battues*, the practice of driving huge herds of animals into a net, something noble Inca hunters did in the mountains. The Caranqui were driven into the swamps and massacred.

Work began to reconstruct the Caranqui fortress as an Inca provincial center. The area was repeopled with loyal subjects, and the north was once again secure. But the army had been weakened by several very bloody defeats, and resources from other parts of the empire had been stripped to support the war effort. Huayna Capac had also been out of Cuzco for far too long; Tomebamba had practically become a second Cuzco. And meanwhile, Huáscar, his heir, had been left in Cuzco and had no experience of warfare. And his lack of experience would become a handicap when he faced off against Atahualpa's rebellion.

Chapter 9: Heading Southward

In addition to heading northward, Topa Inca expanded the Inca Empire to the south, conquering the southern and eastern sides of the Andean Plateau and bringing Lake Titicaca and the former site of the Tihuanaco culture fully into the empire. (At that point, the Tihuanaco culture was only three hundred years in the past, and the remains of its architecture must have been even more impressive than they are today.)

Pachacuti had already conquered the Colla, but he had been too severe with them. As soon as he was dead, they shook their Inca shackles loose again. Topa Inca had to bring reinforcements back from the north to counter their rebellion, which he did very convincingly. The Collas to the north of Lake Titicaca saw their army exterminated and their *huacas* hurled into a deep lake. After seeing this, the Lupacas, who lived to the south of Lake Titicaca, surrendered without resistance.

It must have been at this time that the Titicaca version of the Inca creation myth came into being, with Inti producing Manco Cápac and Mama Ocllo from the lake. To integrate it with the existing story of the Pacaritambo cave, the idea of an underground journey was invoked. The existing idols were replaced. Inti, rather than the Colla golden cat, was made the god of the island Titicaca, while the mother goddess, Mama Quilla, became coupled with Coati Island. The idols of the two gods would visit each other's islands ritually from time to time.

The Collas' territory was now more thoroughly occupied. Many natives were deported, and deserted villages were repopulated. Forty-two different tribes or nations from the rest of Tahuantinsuyu were relocated to this area, creating a cosmopolitan community in which Inca values would predominate or, at least, one where Colla and Lupaca values would be highly diluted.

However, farther east lay problems. The Amazon Basin is completely different from the lands west of the Andes. First of all, it is very wet since the prevailing winds ensure that precipitation falls on the eastern side of the mountains. Secondly, it is covered in thick forest, an environment completely alien to the Inca and the other peoples of their empire. An Amazon tribesman with a bow and arrow could shoot at Inca soldiers without being seen, and making roads was difficult or impossible. And there were, as far as it is known, no urban cultures. The Inca certainly could not fight their preferred kind of warfare in the Amazon.

The presence of the jungle in the east forced them to go farther north and south. This ended up forcing the empire into the straitjacket of a thin strip of land that was thousands of miles long and connected by two main north-south roads like a ladder with a number of rungs between them, connecting inland cities to the coast. The Inca made it as far as the Maule River in Chile. There, they were defeated by the Mapuche, who still populate Chile and Argentina today. This was the farthest south the Inca ever reached.

Chapter 10: Pizarro's Arrival

The Spanish arrived in Latin America from the north. Hernán Cortés spent time on the Caribbean islands of Hispaniola and Cuba. In 1519, he took an expedition to the mainland, crossing Mexico, and in 1521, he took the Aztec capital of Tenochtitlan. He made himself wealthy on Aztec gold and established New Spain, with its capital, Mexico City, on the site of the destroyed Tenochtitlan.

However, not everyone was happy to see Cortés make himself a rich man. Spanish conquistador Francisco Pizarro was looking for his own fortune along with his partner, Diego de Almagro. They had heard rumors of a wealthy country south of Panama where there was a great deal of gold, and they decided to set out to find it.

Their first expedition in 1524 was a failure, but the second expedition in 1526 was more interesting. Pizarro was left on his own, as Almagro had gone back to Panama for supplies, but his pilot, Bartolomé Ruiz, who had continued down the coast to the south, met local traders from Tumbez on a raft wearing fine clothes and gold and silver ornaments. They explained to him that the gold came from far to the south. The stories were true, or so it seemed, and he told Pizarro about them on his return.

However, Pizarro could not find the treasure, and the conditions were tough. Snakes, disease, and malnutrition were picking off his men. So, Pizarro let those who wanted to leave go back to Panama. Meanwhile, he waited with thirteen men for Almagro to come back with provisions. (Things became more complicated when the governor of Panama decided to command the abandonment of the expedition, but Cortés had previously set a precedent when he ignored the governor of Cuba and set off for Mexico. Pizarro and Almagro also decided to ignore the authorities.) When Almagro sent a ship to pick them up, together with new recruits, Pizarro decided to head south toward Tumbez, where he arrived in 1528.

The Spanish were given a warm welcome in Tumbez, and the men Pizarro sent to reconnoiter the city reported seeing people wearing gold and silver. The men also brought news of "little camels" (llamas). Pizarro also heard reports of a mighty empire to the south and was convinced the wealth of Tumbez was a sign that the empire would be even richer and worth taking.

Pizarro headed back north to Panama to find a larger force than his handful of men. But he had a major problem: the governor refused to allow another expedition to the south. Pizarro either had to give up or appeal to a higher authority, which meant sailing for Spain. So, everything was put on hold while Pizarro made his way to Seville, then Toledo. He finally gained a royal license authorizing him to proceed with the conquest of Peru.

Pizarro raised forces in Spain, taking his brothers, half-brothers, and their retainers with him. This time, he had a good story to tell, and he took a good couple of hundred men and a number of horses with him. He landed back in Peru in 1531.

This time, Pizarro did not find a warm welcome in Tumbez. The Inca clearly had information that made them suspicious of the Spanish. So, Pizarro sailed for the island of Puná in the Gulf of Guayaquil and made camp. At first, there was no problem, but Pizarro's interpreters warned him that some of the chiefs of Puná were planning to attack the Spanish. This may or may not have been true, but Pizarro could not afford to ignore the tip. He interrogated the chiefs, satisfied himself that they were guilty, and shipped them to their enemies at Tumbez, where they were put to death.

This did not endear him to the other inhabitants of Tumbez. By acting against the chiefs, Pizarro had precipitated the war he might have avoided. The Spanish camp was charged by thousands of warriors from Puná. However, the Spanish were masters in the use of the pike. Pizarro lined up his pikemen and ordered them to lower their pikes. The enemy warriors ran headlong into the steel blades. A subsequent cavalry attack routed the enemy warriors.

Pizarro next planned how he would take the interior. However, his force was tiny compared to the vast Inca army. Still, Pizarro had two big advantages: horses, which the Inca had never seen, and firearms.

At this point, the Inca were still a Bronze Age people who went to war with clubs, spears, bolas, and slingshots. Their slingshots were remarkably accurate and destructive, and the bolas could bring down a horse easily by wrapping around its legs. If the Inca had been united and able to overcome their panic at facing weapons they didn't understand, they might have been able to destroy Pizarro's entire force. However, fear of the mysterious people (or possibly gods) was a major handicap.

Pizarro also had more advantages. First was a weapon so secret that even Pizarro might not have realized it was fighting on his side: disease. Huayna Capac, who was in Tomebamba, had already received messages from Cuzco that Inca nobles were dying of a plague while also hearing reports of bearded men arriving on the Ecuadorean coast. (Andean indigenous men are very rarely bearded, so this was considered strange.) The plague had also arrived in Quito.

What was it? The Spanish brought various diseases with them to which the indigenous population didn't have even the qualified immunity that the Europeans possessed. Smallpox was one, but there were others, such as measles and typhus.

The second advantage Pizarro had was that Huayna Capac's attempts at changing the way the empire worked had thoroughly destabilized the Inca. He had made the north of Ecuador a separate border region with its own forces to spearhead further advances into the north, but this practically broke the empire in two. (Later, this would enable Atahualpa to make his initial claim to the north.)

Huayna Capac also disinherited Huáscar, who was still in Cuzco, and made Ninan Cuyochi his heir instead. This last decision removed the one source of stability that was left. And when Huayna Capac fell sick with one of the new foreign diseases and died, and then Ninan Cuyochi died from smallpox as well, the Inca Empire was left with no Sapa Inca but had two possible rivals. There was the young and inexperienced Huáscar in Cuzco, and there was the illegitimate but war-hardened Atahualpa in the north. This was the beginning of the Inca Civil War.

Chapter 11: The Inca Civil War

The Inca king list suggests that prior to this date, there had never been any major difficulty in the succession. However, this gives a deceptively simple view of Inca history. The succession appears to have been disputed quite often. Some *auqui* (crown princes) may have been assassinated or poisoned; Pachacuti's successful coup might have been matched by a number of attempted coups of which we have no record.

Huayna Capac was apparently the target of a plot by his regent Hualpay to kill him and take his place as Sapa Inca. Fortunately, Huayna Capac's uncle Huaman Achachi discovered the plot, lured Hualpay's men into the open, and had them killed when they made their attempt on Huayna Capac's life. Hualpay was then executed.

The Inca nobility was small but divided into different factions; the *panacas*, in particular, must have fought for influence against each other. Pachacuti wanted the *panacas* to unify the empire, but they were dividing it into tiny lands of privilege and conspiracy. So, we should not necessarily see the civil war that broke out as exceptional; what *was* truly exceptional was that the European invaders were able to take advantage of the Incas' disarray.

Like all Sapa Incas, Huayna Capac had numerous wives and offspring. His first coya was his full sister, Cusirimay, but she had no sons and appeared to have died early in his reign. He then married another one of his full sisters, Rahua Ocllo. Their son Huáscar was in Cuzco. Huayna Capac's eldest son, Ninan Cuyochi ("Fire Shaker"), had been made Huayna Capac's official heir, but the appointment had not been confirmed. Besides, Ninan Cuyochi died around the same time as Huayna Capac.

Huayna Capac had an illegitimate son by a concubine, probably Tocto Coca. Like Ninan Cuyochi, Atahualpa was favored by Huayna Capac and accompanied his father on his northern campaign. Other sons included Tupac Huallpa (the first "puppet Inca" of the Spanish era), Manco Inca (who would later rebel against the Spanish), and Paullu Inca (who was installed as the Sapa Inca after Manco's rebellion). This wealth of offspring meant that the Inca line was unlikely to die out, but it also delivered far too many potentially competing heirs.

At the time of Huayna Capac's death, Atahualpa and Ninan Cuyochi were with him at Quito, leaving Huáscar in charge of Cuzco. We'll never know what would have happened if Ninan Cuyochi had survived and been able to take charge of the empire unopposed; perhaps he would have been able to bring the empire back to stability. Instead, the empire started to rip itself apart.

The first to move appears to have been Huáscar. He appointed his own priests to perform his coronation and brought his sister, Chuqui Huipa, back from Quito so that he could marry her as his coya. He also purged the executors of Huayna Capac's will, appointed his own council, and eradicated any opposition in Cuzco.

Atahualpa was probably suspicious that Huáscar would turn against him too. As the leader of the northern troops in Quito, he accompanied his father's mummy as far as Tomebamba but then turned back to the north. This was an unprecedented act of desertion.

Atahualpa claimed that his father had split the empire in two, with capitals at Tomebamba and Cuzco, and that he was the legitimate heir to the north. Showing his claim to be a true Sapa Inca, he immediately started building a royal palace in Tomebamba, which was intended to be the first step in creating his own *panaca*.

Huáscar realized he had to rid himself of Atahualpa; otherwise, he would be in serious trouble. He sent his ambassador Atoc (Fox) to the north, and Atoc convinced the Cañari to rebel. They made an attempt on Atahualpa's life, which did not succeed. However, Atahualpa was captured and imprisoned in Tomebamba. He managed to escape again, and this time, he knew he had to beat Huáscar or die.

Atahualpa was already creating his own mythology. He told the story that Inti had appeared to him and turned him into a snake so that he could escape. It is more likely that he managed to break a hole in the wall with a crowbar that a woman brought to him during the inevitable chicha drinking that followed his recapture. The success of this new myth is a warning not to rely on accounts of this period as "true history." Most of the Inca who talked to the Spanish chroniclers would have been on one side or another of the conflict and given the view from that side. In fact, chroniclers can't even agree on who Atahualpa's mother was or whether he was born in Quito or Cuzco.

Table: Whose son was Atahualpa, and where was he born?

Chronicler	What they say
Juan de Betanzos	Atahualpa was born in Cuzco to the concubine Palla Coca.
Pedro Cieza de León	Atahualpa was born in Cuzco to a Quilaco princess.
Pedro Sarmiento de Gamboa	Atahualpa's mother was Tocto Coca.
Inca Garcilaso de la Vega	Atahualpa was born in Quito, and his mother was the crown princess of Quito.
Felipe Guaman Poma de Ayala	Atahualpa's mother was a Chachapoya.
Juan de Santa Cruz Pachacuti	Atahualpa's mother was Tocto Coca, and he was born in Cuzco.
Bernabé Cobo	Atahualpa's mother was Tocto Coca, and he was born in Cuzco.
Juan de Velasco	Atahualpa was born in Quito, and his mother was a princess of Quito.

Huáscar has often been portrayed as a weak and spiteful ruler. Betanzos shows him as a tyrant, but Betanzos's wife had previously been married to Atahualpa, so his account is not without bias. According to some accounts, Huáscar may have been a revolutionary. He is quoted as saying that the royal mummies should all be destroyed and that the riches of the *panacas* should be handed over to the state.

This might have been an outburst caused by frustration. It certainly forced many of the nobility into joining Atahualpa's cause. But it might have been a serious recommendation, especially if Huáscar had seen how the increasing concentration of power in *panaca* hands and the requirement for the next Inca to continue expanding the empire were weakening the state.[15] Arguably, the Inca needed to consolidate after the conquests made by Topa Inca. Huayna Capac appears to have spent as much of his time putting down rebellions as actively expanding the empire. Huáscar's solution, had he had time to put it into action and *if* he was serious, might have given the Inca a chance.

In the meantime, Huáscar moved his headquarters from his palace, which was a part of his late father's compound on Haucaypata, to Collcampata, which was outside the city, taking over the land that had formed Manco Cápac's garden. The dead had actually forced out the living; there was no room left on Haucaypata for him to build his own palace since every inch of frontage was occupied by one of the *panacas.*

The Inca Civil War was unavoidable. It was hugely expensive in terms of human resources. The first battle, which was fought at Ambato, may have killed as many as fifteen thousand men; years later, under Spanish rule, the ground was still littered with bones. (Atoc was apparently killed in this battle, and Atahualpa made his skull into a gilded drinking cup.) Atahualpa quickly proceeded to take Tomebamba and massacred the Cañari who stood against him. He then destroyed the city and leveled its walls, thus destroying one of the best fortresses in the north.

Huáscar remained in Cuzco and sent his half-brother and general Huanca Auqui to do battle on his behalf. Huanca Auqui had already

[15] Brundage, Burr Cartwright. *Empire of the Inca.* Pg. 267.

lost Tomebamba, and he continued his losing streak at Cochahuayla. He had a weak point: the Chachapoya levies from the eastern side of the Andes. And Atahualpa noticed. By concentrating his forces on the Chachapoya, Atahualpa defeated Huanca Auqui's army. Cajamarca now lay open to Atahualpa, and he moved his headquarters there.

Atahualpa stayed in Cajamarca, but his army pressed on under generals Quizquiz and Chalcuchímac. At Jauja, there was a massive battle, and again, Huáscar's side lost. Mayca Yupanqui, who was appointed leader of the army by Huáscar to replace Huanca Auqui, was just as unsuccessful as his predecessor and had to retreat while being pursued by Atahualpa's troops. At this point, Huáscar decided to leave Cuzco and lead his army personally.

Huáscar was on the back foot, but at Cotapampa, he had a sudden change of fortune. One of his war leaders managed to isolate and destroy Atahualpa's advance guard, and Huáscar was able to move his army up to the pass of Cotapampa, barring Atahualpa's way. However, Atahualpa's generals were too smart for Huáscar. They anticipated that Huáscar would employ the typical Inca stratagem of trying to flank the opposing army, so they lay in wait for the flanking parties, killed them, and then created an ambush. When Huáscar's center attacked, they found enemies on both sides. Huáscar made a run for Cuzco, but the road to Cuzco was now open to Atahualpa's army.

Quizquiz took possession of Cuzco and immediately started a purge of Huáscar's supporters. Huanca Auqui and his men, together with the priests who had crowned Huáscar, were immediately taken out. Rocks were dropped on their backs, maiming but not killing them, which was the punishment for common crimes and an immensely disrespectful way to treat pure-blooded Inca. Atahualpa sent word from Cota Pampa, his headquarters in the north, to kill all of Huáscar's kin and supporters, including his eighty children and any concubines who were pregnant. Two of his sisters, the mothers of his children, were also killed. Thirty of his brothers were massacred, with Huáscar being compelled to witness the act.

Since Huáscar had been linked to his grandfather Topa Inca's *panaca*, the members of that household were also killed, and the mummy of Topa Inca was taken out and burned. Atahualpa had practically extinguished the legitimate line. Quizquiz had also done exactly what Huáscar had spoken about, destroying a Sapa Inca's mummy and *panaca*. All of Huáscar's quipus were burned, destroying all memory of his rule (or, at least, Quizquiz must have hoped) and also destroying the machinery by which the empire was governed.

This massacre of a great part of the ruling class, together with the destruction of huge amounts of data, deprived the empire of a large part of its administrative ability. Atahualpa had exterminated the opposition to his rule, but he had also made Pizarro's task much easier. The invincible Inca war machine was now falling apart.

Chapter 12: Atahualpa's Death

Atahualpa had now become Sapa Inca, but he was still in the north at Cajamarca. He was probably making plans to head to Cuzco to be crowned, but he never had the chance.

Pizarro brought his troops inland and approached Cajamarca. Atahualpa appears not to have believed that he had anything to fear from the small Spanish band. He had eighty thousand men camped outside the city, and Pizarro had a couple of hundred men in total. Atahualpa perhaps deliberately lured Pizarro into the mountains, hoping to pick the Spanish off at some point, but so far, Pizarro had not posed any threat. Otherwise, Atahualpa was disastrously over-confident and had decided that he did not need to defend the passes against this ragtag band of men. If he had made a stand anywhere along Pizarro's route, the Inca surely would have won.

Pizarro was in a bind. He could not go back, he could not go forward, and he was surrounded by superior forces. He decided to gamble everything on one throw of the dice. On Friday, November 11th, 1532, he arrived in Cajamarca. The town was almost empty, with most of the Inca having joined Atahualpa's forces. Pizarro invited Atahualpa to meet with him.

Atahualpa waited for dusk. Apparently, many of the Inca believed that horses were inoperative at night since they had never seen horses moving after sunset. He took seven thousand of his troops but armed them with only ceremonial battle axes and small knives. His attendants were richly dressed, and Atahualpa was carried in a litter.

He evidently expected the tactics that had worked for Huayna Capac at Jauja to work for him now: impressing the enemy with the civilization, wealth, and generosity of his people to win them over.

Unfortunately, the Spanish had other plans. Many of them had hidden in the tight alleyways that surrounded the open space of the main square or inside buildings. Four small cannons had also been hidden inside a small building. And there, the Spanish waited in complete silence, some of them terrified of what could turn out to be their last battle.

When the Inca arrived, the town seemed to be empty. Then Fra Vicente de Valverde, the Spanish priest, emerged from one of the buildings with an interpreter. He approached Atahualpa and demanded that Atahualpa accept Catholicism and Charles V of Spain as his ruler. Atahualpa probably was never going to accept these conditions, but apparently, there was some discussion of what certain terms meant. Then, according to some accounts, Fra Vicente gave Atahualpa a Bible, which the Inca ruler threw to the ground.

At this point, the guns began to fire. This was the signal for the hidden Spanish forces to launch the attack. The exits from the square were blocked, and the Inca now experienced two things they had never seen before: a cavalry attack and gunfire. Atahualpa sat immobile as the charge launched directly at him.

Some two to three thousand Inca warriors were killed in Cajamarca that night. Atahualpa was very nearly killed, but Pizarro realized his usefulness as a hostage, so he blocked the attack on him by another soldier, getting wounded in the process. Some survivors made it out of Cajamarca by breaking down part of the walls.

* * *

The account from Titu Cusi Yupanqui, son of Manco Cápac II, was slightly different. According to him, Atahualpa had received two of the Spanish sometime before the Battle of Cajamarca while relations were still friendly. (It's interesting that Titu Cusi calls them "two Viracochas," referring to the idea that the Spanish represented the return of the absent creator god from his retreat under the sea.)

Atahualpa offered Pizarro and his companion Hernando de Soto a cup containing chicha. To the Inca, chicha was a ceremonial drink and often a sacrificial offering; it was, so to speak, holy, just as holy as the Bible that Atahualpa had thrown to the ground. The Spanish clearly had not encountered anything as disgusting as this beer and tipped it out. This action was a dreadful insult.

According to Titu Cusi, at this meeting, one of the Spaniards tried to give Atahualpa "a writing," which they said was the word of God and the Spanish king. Remember, the Inca were not literate, so Atahualpa could not have understood what he was supposed to do with the paper. Titu Cusi, who was baptized into the Catholic Church as Don Diego de Castro, understood what writing represented but was not specific about the nature of the text.

Titu Cusi says that the shooting in Cajamarca started when Atahualpa yelled, "If you disrespect me, I will disrespect you."

* * *

Now that Pizarro had Atahualpa in his hands, the remaining Inca army simply melted away. They had seen fewer than two hundred men kill their Sapa Inca and his bodyguards; no doubt some of them believed that the "Viracochas" were actually gods of some sort. The Inca also had no leader. They must have felt powerless.

Pizarro saw his chance at obtaining riches. He held an emperor who owned an immense store of wealth, so he demanded a ransom. Pizarro said Atahualpa would be allowed to go once he filled a room once with gold and twice with silver. Anthropologist Gordon McEwan gives an estimate of 13,420 pounds of gold and 26,000 pounds of silver; the gold alone would be worth $230 million today.[16] This may well be the reason Coricancha was stripped of its gold plate.

It's not always easy to work out the precise order in which things happen. What is known is that Atahualpa ordered the murder of Huáscar, perhaps thinking Huáscar could pay Pizarro more than the ransom. And who knows what Huáscar would do once he got his hands on his rival? But one account says Atahualpa had already raised the issue with Pizarro, telling Pizarro that one of his men had killed Huáscar against his orders. Pizarro reassured Atahualpa that this would change nothing in the contract between them, giving Atahualpa full assurance that he could murder Huáscar with impunity, and so he gave the order, which was carried out in Cuzco.

---

[16] McEwan, Gordon F. *The Inca: New Perspectives.* Pg. 21,

However, killing his rival did Atahualpa no good. It is possible that Pizarro had never intended to free the imprisoned Inca once he got his hands on the ransom. It is also possible that Pizarro wanted to get out of Cajamarca quickly because Almagro, who had earlier been left behind, had now arrived, and Almagro wanted some of the loot. Almagro advocated killing Atahualpa fast, and though Hernando Pizarro (Francisco's brother) and Hernando de Soto wanted to save the Inca's life, they were overruled. There were also accusations that Atahualpa, though a prisoner, had been raising armies to attack the Spanish through intermediaries. Whatever the reason, Atahualpa was doomed.

But his murder had to be given some form of legitimacy. A kangaroo court was convened, and Atahualpa was brought to face charges of murder (of Huáscar), idolatry, and rebellion against Spanish rule. He was condemned to be burned at the stake.

In a society where the dead were pampered and respected, this was a horrifying fate. If Atahualpa were burned, he would not have a mummy and would not enjoy the benefits of his next stage of existence. He was told that if he converted to Catholicism, he could be garroted instead, which meant his body would survive. He was baptized by Fra Vicente de Valverde and given the name Francisco in honor of Pizarro.

Don Francisco Atahualpa was executed on July 26th, 1533.

* * *

After Atahualpa, the empire fell apart. A major problem was the fact that initiative was not rewarded in the Inca Empire. It was a society in which doing the job that was required in one's given role was the gold standard. Without the Sapa Inca to give directions, there was nothing left.

Some of the subject people willingly backed the Spanish. Both Huáscar and Atahualpa probably would have been surprised by the sheer amount of hatred that many of their subjects had for the Inca. While in the early days of the empire, subject people generally benefited from a certain reciprocity, giving their labor as tax but in return receiving cloth, food when the harvest failed, and security, under Huayna Capac (and perhaps even earlier), the empire had been demanding more and more and delivering less and less. The empire was already, to some extent, broken before Pizarro came.

A few individual warlords took advantage of the empire's fragmentation. Rumiñahui ("Stone Face"), one of Atahualpa's generals, led a resistance in the north for two years but was eventually captured. Before he was captured, though, he hid all the treasures of Quito and killed the *aclla* who refused to escape so that they would not be taken by the Spanish. He also set Quito on fire. The Spanish, naturally, were most interested in the hidden treasure, but although they tortured Rumiñahui, he never gave his secret away.

Quizquiz, Atahualpa's trusted general, led his troops to the safety of the mountains, but the fragile links that held the army together broke, and his troops, arguing that it was planting season and that they needed to go home, killed him and disappeared.

Chapter 13: Last Stand of the Inca

Pizarro felt that he needed a puppet Inca to rule the empire. He simply did not have the resources to administer it, and he must have been aware that he was still playing a gigantic confidence trick. He could not afford his bluff to be called.

Fortunately, Huayna Capac had been a highly prolific procreator, so there were plenty of candidates. First, Pizarro had Tupac Huallpa consecrated as the Sapa Inca. All of the ceremonies were carried out in an attempt to legitimize the puppet ruler. However, Tupac Huallpa died within a few months.

However, Tupac Huallpa played an important part in Inca history, albeit in an indirect way. He had at least four children, one of whom was Palla Chimpu Ocllo. She was baptized as Isabel, married a Spaniard, and was the mother of Inca Garcilaso de la Vega, who emigrated to Spain and wrote one of the best-known chronicles of the Inca Empire.

After Tupac Inca's death, another son of Huayna Capac was found: Manco Inca Yupanqui. This half-brother of Huáscar had somehow managed to escape the massacres ordered by Atahualpa and was crowned in Cuzco.

Almagro and Pizarro divided the country. Almagro took Cuzco, while Pizarro took the northern part of Peru. But Almagro had been on an expedition south to Chile; meanwhile, the Pizarros looted Cuzco, thinking Manco Inca would not stand in their way.

However, Manco Inca was not the puppet that Pizarro wanted. In 1535, he tried to escape Cuzco, but he was caught and put in prison. Stupidly, Pizarro's younger brothers, Gonzalo and Juan, who he'd left in charge of Cuzco while pursuing remnants of the Inca army elsewhere, decided it would be a good idea to send Manco Inca to recover a golden statue of Huayna Capac from his estate in the Yucay Valley with only a couple of men to look after him. Once again, gold had turned Spanish minds. Manco Inca easily escaped again, and this time, he was not recaptured.

Manco Cápac II, as he came to be called by some of his followers, easily raised a large number of troops. He laid siege to Cuzco in 1536. The siege lasted ten months. Manco Inca may have had anywhere between 40,000 and 200,000 Inca under his command against 180 Spanish defenders.

The Inca first seized the huge fortress of Sacsayhuaman above Cuzco, a well-fortified position from which they could launch attacks on the city. The very steep slopes meant the Spanish could not use one of their main advantages, the cavalry, as horses could not cope with the terrain. The Inca used slings to launch burning projectiles into the city, igniting the thatched roofs of the houses. The fire quickly spread. Cavalry sorties on the flat land around the city were met by bolas, which entangled the horses' feet.

At the same time, Manco Inca sent Quizu Yupanqui to march on Lima, the newly founded capital. Several rescue parties were sent by the Spanish from Lima to try to liberate Cuzco, but four were caught and destroyed by Quizu Yupanqui, and the fifth retreated before he could get to them. Quizu Yupanqui was then ordered to attack Lima.

Lima was not the easy target Manco Inca thought it would be. There were very few Spaniards there, perhaps about five hundred, against a strong Inca force, but the Spanish were helped by more than four thousand indigenous *curacas* and servants, including Huancas and other tribes that resisted Inca rule. Many of them had been equipped with swords. Also, while Manco Inca and Quizu Yupanqui were experts at using mountain terrain strategically, the area around Lima was largely flat. This gave the Spanish cavalry a big advantage.

The siege lasted for six days, with Lima being almost completely surrounded by Inca troops. On the sixth day, Quizu Yupanqui was impatient and decided to make a major assault on the city. The Spanish, who were mounted on their steeds and waiting inside the city, let the Inca come into the streets and then charged them. Quizu Yupanqui's troops were routed, and seeing this, his remaining captains fled.

Peruvian archaeologists Guillermo Cock and Elena Goycochea excavated bodies at a cemetery near Lima that had been buried without the usual Inca wrappings and bore evidence of violent wounds, including a gunshot. There were also indications of trauma from blunt weapons, such as maces and clubs, that would have been used by the indigenous defenders.[17]

Despite the lack of help from Lima, Cuzco held out. Eventually, the Spanish reconquered Sacsayhuaman by first distracting many of the defenders with a feigned cavalry "escape" toward Lima and then mounting a night attack using scaling ladders. This eased the pressure, and after ten months of inconclusive fighting, Manco Inca withdrew to Ollantaytambo and then to Vilcabamba. Here, he established what is called the Neo-Inca state, which was defended not so much by his army as by the very difficult terrain. (Hiram Bingham, by the way, thought Machu Picchu was Manco Inca's capital. However, this has turned out not to be the case.)

Meanwhile, Pizarro found another son of Huayna Capac, Paullu Inca, and installed him as a puppet ruler. Paullu converted to Catholicism, and his son, Carlos Inca, was thoroughly Hispanicized.

But the Pizarros had thoroughly looted Cuzco, which was meant to be Almagro's domain. Soon the Spanish were effectively locked in a civil war between Almagro's and Pizarro's supporters. Almagro and Francisco Pizarro were both killed as a direct result of the conflict. This, together with the small size of the Spanish forces, gave Manco Inca a second chance. But while he had decided on a major siege in 1536, in 1537, he decided instead to engage in what we would now call a guerrilla war. Small groups of Spaniards traveling through Peru were attacked and killed, and isolated garrisons were attacked by local

---

[17] Wilford, John Noble. "New World's first gunshot victim is uncovered in Peru." New York Times, June 19, 2007.

forces loyal to the Neo-Inca state. There was no big army for the Spanish to chase down; the guerrillas melted away into the mountains.

However, although Peru became an increasingly dangerous place, and the death toll continued to rise, Manco Inca could not achieve any major success.

The Neo-Inca state seems to have flourished in its little enclave, though, so much so that a number of Spanish outlaws who had fallen out of favor headed for Vilcabamba. Manco Inca gladly gave them refuge upon learning that several of them had been involved in the assassination of Francisco Pizarro. Pizarro had once kidnapped, tortured, and killed Manco Inca's sister-wife, Cura Ocllo; now, Manco Inca could display his gratitude to the men who had killed his wife's murderer.

However, that turned out to be a mistake. One day, a Spaniard was playing a game of horseshoes with Manco Inca and got into an argument with him. The Spaniard picked up a horseshoe and hammered Manco Inca's head with it. An alternative version is that the Spaniards conspired to assassinate Manco Inca, hoping that the Spanish authorities would pardon them as a reward.

Their treachery did not pay off. They were captured and killed by the Inca soldiers.

Manco Inca had been a man of vision. For instance, he planned to train his men in Spanish ways of fighting with firearms, armor, and swords. However, after his death, the training was abandoned.

Sayri Tupac, Manco Inca's son, took over the title of Sapa Inca in 1544. He was only nine years old and reigned with the aid of regents. The Spanish, now with a viceroy installed in Lima, saw the chance to secure peace. Sayri Tupac was offered property in Cuzco and a privileged lifestyle if he was prepared to abandon Vilcabamba. He accepted and was already preparing to move when Paullu Inca (the other Sapa Inca backed by the Spanish) suddenly died. Upon hearing this, Sayri Tupac had second thoughts.

Another offer was made to Sayri Tupac in 1556. Eventually, he agreed to leave Vilcabamba, convert to Catholicism, and accept an estate in the Yucay Valley. Don Diego, as he now was known, received a special dispensation from the pope to marry his sister and settled down to domestic life in the most pleasant and green landscapes Peru had to offer. But he died in his twenties in 1561. Rumor has it that he was poisoned.

His half-brother, Titu Cusi Yupanqui, seized the throne back in Vilcabamba and lived by brigandage for a while, although he eventually negotiated peace and became a Catholic. He is a particularly interesting figure because he narrated the story of the Spanish invasion, his father's murder, and his own life to the Spanish missionary named Fray Marcos García.

Titu Cusi died in 1571, apparently of pneumonia. However, the Inca were convinced that he had been poisoned. His scribe, Martin Pando, was caught and immediately killed. The Augustinian friar Diego Ortiz was kept alive for a while but was eventually executed as well.

This left Tupac Amaru, another son of Manco Inca, as the new Sapa Inca. He had not converted. Titu Cusi had made him the keeper of Manco Inca's mummy, and he had been living in the temple at Vilcabamba. Therefore, he had no experience of war or politics. This was all the more serious since he had to cope with a new viceroy, Francisco de Toledo, Count of Oropesa, who was much stricter than previous viceroys and introduced new policies. Toledo started the *reducciones*, the process of moving Inca subjects off their fields and into newly built towns.

De Toledo must have seen the existence of the Neo-Inca state as intolerable. The Spanish could not be secure as long as it continued to exist. But he needed an excuse for taking action, and he was given it by one of Tupac Amaru's captains. The Spanish sent two ambassadors to negotiate with Titu Cusi, news of whose death had not yet reached Lima. They were both killed on the border of Vilcabamba territory. De Toledo declared war in 1572. Vilcabamba was under siege.

Manco Inca had been smart enough to hold back the Spanish from crossing the river into Vilcabamba territory. Tupac Amaru did not have great military experience, so he was less prudent. But he was in a winning position, as his troops were all within Vilcabamba while the Spanish were on the other side of a rope bridge so narrow that only one man could pass at a time. All the Inca had to do was wait and pick off the attackers one by one.

However, the Spanish had a small cannon with them, and they opened fire. This apparently terrified the Inca, and Tupac Amaru fled with his troops into the jungle but left the bridge intact. This gave the Spanish access to the Neo-Inca domain. Eventually, Tupac Amaru was found and was persuaded to surrender after he was promised that no harm would come to him.

Of course, this was a lie. Tupac Amaru was put on trial, accused of ordering the murder of the priests after Titu Cusi's death, and sentenced to be beheaded. He is said by some writers to have accepted baptism before his execution, but his last words do not bear this out. According to archaeologist James Q. Jacobs, Tupac Amaru's final words from the scaffold were "Collanan Pachacamac ricuy auccacuna yahuarniy hichcascancuta," a direct appeal to the creator: "Witness how my enemies shed my blood."

Tupac Amaru's head was put on a pike by the Spanish. They did not expect what happened next, though; the Inca began to worship it. It had to be taken down quickly and buried with the body in the church of San Domingo, which had been built on top of the Coricancha sun temple.

And this was the end of the Inca. Up to 1572, life had been very similar for many of the subjects of the Inca Empire. They continued to inhabit their villages and perform their regular tasks. Low-level *curacas* simply became foremen in the colonial bureaucracy.

But things changed dramatically after this. Spain had already transformed Peru from an outlaw state run by mercenaries to a Spanish dependency run by viceroys; now, it had to be even further changed to bring it in line with the European model of society. The viceroy broke up the villages, created new towns, and forcibly removed people from their fields into the townships. The *ayllus* were broken up. European crops were brought in, as well as sugarcane.

And the ancestor mummies were burned. The mummies of Manco Inca and Titu Cusi were brought from Vilcabamba, and these along with any remaining mummies in Cuzco and all the *huacas* that survived were destroyed by burning. The Inca had still been venerating the mummies up to the 1560s, but the Spanish were becoming increasingly intolerant. This was not only the destruction of a ceremonial practice, though; it was the destruction of history.

Remember, Inca history was recited in front of the mummies, keeping their oral history alive. Once the Spanish destroyed the mummies and their cult, they also destroyed the chief way in which the Inca guarded their history. Effectively, they had destroyed the Inca identity.

* * *

Tupac Amaru was not the last of the Inca. His death marked the end of the Inca Empire, but not the end of the Inca. The Inca people survived, though many were enslaved. Others converted and married the Spanish.

In 1780, there was a strange footnote in Inca history. José Gabriel Condorcanqui, an indigenous leader, was a Jesuit-educated, upwardly mobile trader who inherited the leadership of several villages from his father. The late 1770s were bad years for traders, with overproduction pushing prices down and Lima creating a monopoly on many goods. Merchants started going bankrupt. New customs charges and other taxes were taking an increasing bite of any profit that was left.

Condorcanqui knew that he was descended from royal Inca blood. He adopted the name of Tupac Amaru II, honoring his ancestor, and started a judicial process for official recognition of his lineage, which was eventually refused. He saw how the poor Inca were being exploited through forced labor and extortion from Catholic priests. He appealed time and again for these unfortunates, but no one listened. Eventually, he decided a revolution was the only way to change things for the Inca people—*his* people.

On November 4th, 1780, Governor Antonio de Arriaga attended a banquet with, among others, Tupac Amaru. Arriaga left the party drunk; he was captured, and his slave was given the privilege of hanging him. After assembling a six-thousand-strong army, Tupac Amaru set off for Cuzco, with his men looting Spanish houses and killing any Spaniards they found.

But Tupac Amaru failed to capture Cuzco. He spent too much time touring the provinces and building up a larger army when he should have marched directly for the capital. In the end, two of his officers turned on him. He was sentenced to be executed and had to watch the execution of his wife, son, uncle, and a number of his captains before meeting his own death.

The place of his execution was Haucaypata, the main square of Cuzco. This was the place where the mummies of his ancestors had once been displayed and where Tupac Amaru I had also been executed.

Conclusion

The Inca Empire was an amazing episode in history. From an unpromising, difficult terrain and a small-scale tribal culture sprang a huge and remarkably well-administered empire, which grew from a city-state to an empire in the space of just a hundred years and then dramatically fell. For a preliterate culture that was still in the Bronze Age, this was a truly remarkable accomplishment.

While other civilizations in the region, such as the Huari and Tihuanaco, had started to develop terraced agriculture, road networks, and stone architecture, the Inca brought these developments to an unprecedented height. One of the factors that helped the empire greatly was its willingness to integrate the artistic and technological strengths of the people it conquered. Bringing craftsmen to Cuzco and moving populations around the empire to spread agricultural techniques and new varieties of crops accelerated development and boosted productivity.

When earlier cultures in the same region are considered, the speed with which the Inca grew appears even more exceptional. Tihuanaco lasted six centuries, as did the Huari; the Moche lasted seven centuries, and the Chimú nearly five hundred. The Inca didn't make it past four centuries and yet came to dominate an area several times larger than any of the previous cultures. You could say the Inca were Andeans on steroids.

However, the empire held the seeds of its own destruction. The *panaca* system, which preserved the Sapa Inca's personal estate and forced the new ruler to build his own wealth through conquest, put the state on a path of expansion that could not be slowed or stopped. This was responsible for the empire's initial fast growth, but by the early 16th century, the Inca did not have enough resources to pacify and integrate all of the recently conquered peoples. The suppression of rebellions took more time than actual conquest, and the empire had become too large for the administration.

The class-based nature of the administrative system and the fact that pure-blooded Inca were in the minority led to increasing tension with the subject peoples. At the same time, the *panaca* system generated increasing factionalism among the Inca nobility. By the time the Spanish arrived in South America, the empire was already showing the strain; it had to change or go under. Francisco Pizarro simply tipped the scales.

But the Inca did not disappear. Their traditions survived in Peru, even though the Spanish attempted to uproot all traces of native religions. For instance, shrines of the Virgin Mary have often taken over the site of a spring or temple dedicated to Pachamama or Mama Quilla, for instance, at Copacabana on Lake Titicaca. Many of the saints took on the colors of the Inca gods; for instance, Saint James absorbed many of the symbols of the thunder god Illapa.

The Inca also accomplished another thing that changed the region forever. They had spread the Quechua language across a huge area. In fact, that may have made the work of the Spanish much easier since they could use a single Quechua interpreter instead of needing several interpreters to speak all the different local languages.

Today, Quechua is spoken by more than eight million people across six different countries. In 1975, it was declared an official language in Peru. Former President Evo Morales of Bolivia promoted Quechua and Aymara teaching in schools, and Quechua is now used in education within Ecuador, Bolivia, and Peru.

Although many other indigenous peoples had joined the Spanish against the Inca, as time passed, the Inca became a rallying point for those who had suffered prejudice and injustice under Spanish rule. Many natives who were not of Inca blood came to identify with the Inca as indigenous rulers who demonstrated that it was possible for the natives to rule their own land.

Even Hispanics have sometimes adopted Inca coloration for Peruvian nationalist projects. However, this is often tinged with nostalgia for a theoretical "pure" Inca past and does not necessarily indicate any respect for contemporary indigenous cultures or people.

Still, as anthropologist and archaeologist Michael Malpass claims, "Inca culture is very much alive today."[18] Weaving is still one of the major craft traditions in the region, and the looms that are used by weavers have not changed. Many of the patterns are still reminiscent of Inca designs. In some areas, Inca terraces are still being used for agriculture. Some are being rebuilt as local farmers have started to reclaim traditional methods of cultivation.

While Inca cuisine may not have taken over the world (in fact, if you go out to eat in Cuzco, you're likely to find Chinese restaurants to be a popular choice), a number of Inca foodstuffs have become known to consumers elsewhere as interesting and healthy choices. For instance, quinoa has become commonly used as an alternative to other grains in salads and soups. Oca isn't widely available in supermarkets, but a lot of gardeners now grow the tuber. And let's not forget that it was Andean farmers, though maybe not Inca farmers, who were responsible for breeding the potato from a tiny tuber into a viable food crop.

And, of course, the Inca have given Peru a fantastic number of attractions for tourists. Machu Picchu has over 1.5 million visitors a year; 25,000 hikers make their way there on the Inca Trail. The success of tourism has given authorities a headache. Strict limits have had to be imposed on visitor numbers in order to preserve the site.

So, the Inca have definitely left their stamp on the world, even though they couldn't make their empire stay the course.

---

[18] Malpass, Michael A. *Daily Life in the Inca Empire.*

Basic dates in Inca history

1200	Inca recorded in Cuzco
1230-1260	Possible dates for the rule of Sinchi Roca.
1290-1320	Possible dates for the rule of Mayta Cápac.
Early 1400s	Inca living around Cuzco defeat and then integrate other local groups.
	Alliance with Titicaca-based Lupaca to defend the southwest.
1438	The Chanca tribe takes Cuzco from Viracocha Inca. Inca Yupanqui retakes Cuzco and becomes Pachacuti Inca. He then conquers the area to the north of Lake Titicaca.
1460-1463	Topa Inca (Pachacuti's son) conquers coastal regions, northern Peru, and part of Ecuador.
1471	Death of Pachacuti. The rule of Topa Inca begins. Conquests in the south.

1493	Accession of Huayna Capac. The Inca Empire achieves its greatest extent.
1522	Huayna Capac defeats the Caranqui.
1525	Death of Huayna Capac. Accession of Huáscar Inca.
1527	Civil war between Huáscar and Atahualpa.
1531	Pizarro takes the island of Puná.
1533	Atahualpa defeats Huáscar. The Spanish arrive, capture, and kill Atahualpa. Tupac Huallpa is made a puppet ruler by Pizarro.
	Death of Tupac Huallpa and succession of Manco Inca.
1537	Manco Inca's rebellion fails.
1560	Spanish authorities round up most of the royal mummies, ending their cult.
1561	Death of Manco Inca Yupanqui.
1563	Death of Sayri Tupac.
1570	The arrival of Don Francisco de Toledo as viceroy.
1571	Death of Titu Cusi Yupanqui.
1572	Execution of Tupac Amaru, the last Sapa Inca. The destruction of the remaining mummies.

1780	Rebellion led by Tupac Amaru II (José Gabriel Condorcanqui).
1781	Execution of Tupac Amaru II and his wife, Micaela Bastidas.

Here's another book by Enthralling History that you might like

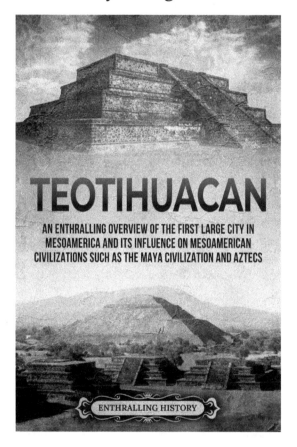

Free limited time bonus

Stop for a moment. We have a free bonus set up for you. The problem is this: we forget 90% of everything that we read after 7 days. Crazy fact, right? Here's the solution: we've created a printable, 1-page pdf summary for this book that you're reading now. All you have to do to get your free pdf summary is to go to the following website:

https://livetolearn.lpages.co/enthrallinghistory/

Once you do, it will be intuitive. Enjoy, and thank you!

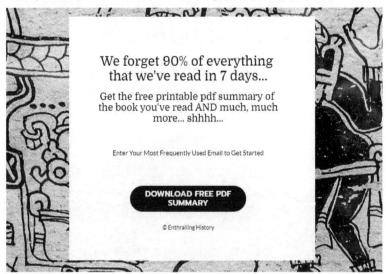

We forget 90% of everything that we've read in 7 days...

Get the free printable pdf summary of the book you've read AND much, much more... shhhh...

Enter Your Most Frequently Used Email to Get Started

DOWNLOAD FREE PDF SUMMARY

© Enthralling History

Glossary

Aclla - a "chosen woman," a non-Inca girl chosen between the ages of seven and ten and trained in an acllahuasi. An aclla might remain in a religious establishment, become a concubine to the Inca, or be gifted to a curaca or Inca noble. Some were sacrificed.

Acllahuasi - a "house of aclla," where the chosen women were trained in weaving, chicha making, and religion.

Amauta - an Inca teacher

Apu - a governor in charge of one of the four quarters of the Inca Empire

Auqui - crown prince; also used as a part of Inca personal names

Ayllu - a clan, the traditional form of social organization in the Andes

Bola - weights attached to connected cords that could be thrown at animals to entangle their feet.

Cancha - a walled compound containing four houses around a courtyard

Chasqui - a runner who carried messages along the roads as part of a relay system, either in the form of quipus or having memorized the message

Chullpa - a funerary house containing the bodies or mummies of the dead

Colca - a storehouse for food and textiles built along the roads and in main population centers

Coya - the sister-wife of the Sapa Inca

Cumbi - the finest grade of woolen cloth, frequently used as a gift or sacrifice

Curaca - a local leader or administrator

Huaca - a sacred place or object. Huacas might include mountain peaks, springs, caves, ancestral mummies, talismans, or places where a Sapa Inca had been born or died.

Inca - specifically, a member of the Inca tribe of Cuzco. May also be used to refer to the Sapa Inca, the ruler of the empire.

Mallqui - a mummy bundle that contained the body of an ancestor wrapped in textiles. The body would be in a seated position. A mallqui was considered still "living," though in a different way, and was a huaca or sacred object.

Mamacona - a woman devoted to the service of a temple

Mascapaicha - the Sapa Inca's fringe of red wool worn on the forehead, which was a sign of his status. The Inca used the term "to take the Mascapaicha" to describe the accession of a new Sapa Inca.

Mitma – the system of displacing people. Families were transferred by the Inca from one territory to another. This might be for various reasons, such as, for instance, the desire to transfer particular skills or to move potentially rebellious people away from their traditional lands.

Moiety - the Inca divided social units and cities into two moieties, a superior and a lower moiety. These would then include a number of different *ayllus*.

Panaca - the estate of a deceased emperor that was administered by his descendants. Its job was to maintain the care of his mummy.

Quechua - the language spoken by the Inca and the language of administration in the Inca Empire

Quipu - a method of recording numbers and other data by means of knotted strings

Sapa Inca – "Unique Inca" or "Only Inca," the ruler of the Inca

Sinchi - a warlord

Suyu - a "quarter" of the Inca Empire

Tambo - rest houses built at regular distances along the major roads of the empire

Tahuantinsuyu - the Land of Four Quarters, the Inca name for the empire

Tucricuc - a senior Inca official

Tupu - (1) a clothespin used to fasten garments; (2) a measure of land enough to feed a childless couple

Yachayhuasi - the school for young men in Cuzco

Yanacona - a servant on an estate

Bibliography

Baudin, Louis. *A Socialist Empire: The Inca of Peru.* D Van Nostrand, Princeton, 1961.

Bingham, Hiram. *Inca Land: Explorations in the Highlands of Peru.* 2003.

Bingham, Hiram. *Lost City of the Inca: The Story of Machu Picchu and its Builders.* Phoenix House, London, 1952.

Brundage, Burr Cartwright. *Empire of the Inca (The Civilization of the American Indian Series).* University of Oklahoma Press, Norman, 1963.

Cobo, Father Bernabe: Hamilton, Roland tr and ed. *History of the Inca Empire: An Account of the Indians' Customs and Their Origin Together with a Treatise on Inca Legends, History and Social Institutions.* University of Texas Press, Austin, 1979.

Conrad, Geoffrey & Demarest, Arthur A. *Religion and Empire: The Dynamics of Aztec and Inca Expansionism.* Cambridge University Press, 1984.

Diamond, Jared. Collapse: *How Societies Choose to Fail or Succeed.* Viking Press, 2005.

Flores Galindo, Alberto. *In Search of an Inca: Identity and Utopia in the Andes.* Cambridge University Press, 2010.

Jacobs, James Q. "Tupac Amaru: The Life, Times and Execution of the Last Inca." http://www.jqjacobs.net/andes/tupac_amaru.html.

Hemming, John. *The Conquest of the Inca.* Harcourt, Brace, Jovanovich, New York, 1970.

Hyslop, John. *Inkawasi the New Cuzco.* British Archaeological Reports, Oxford, 1985.

Kolata, A. (1986). "The Agricultural Foundations of the Tiwanaku State: A View from the Heartland." American Antiquity, 51(4), 748-762.

Locke, L Leland. "A Peruvian Quipu. Contributions from the Museum of the American Indian." Heye Foundation, volume VII number 5. New York, 1927.

Malpass, Michael A. *Daily Life in the Inca Empire.* Greenwood Press, Westport, CT, 1996.

McEwan, Gordon F. *The Inca: New Perspectives.* ABC Clio, Santa Barbara, 2006.

Mead, Charles W. *The Musical Instruments of the Inca.* 1924.

Murra, John Victor. *The Economic Organization of the Inca State.* 1956.

Niles, Susan A. *The Shape of Inca History: Narrative and Architecture in an Andean Empire.* University of Iowa Press, 1999.

Nordenskiold, Erland. *The Secret of the Peruvian Quipus.* 1925.

Pillsbury, Joanne, Patricia Sarro, James Doyle, and Juliet Wiersema. "Design for Eternity: Architectural Models from the Ancient Americas." New York: Metropolitan Museum of Art, 2015.

Rowe, John Howland. *Inca Culture at the Time of the Spanish Conquest.* US Government Printing Office, 1946.

Silverblatt, Irene. *Moon, Sun, and Witches: Gender Ideologies and Class in Inca and Colonial Peru.* Princeton University Press, 1987.

Somervill, Barbara A. *Great Empires of the Past: Empire of the Inca.* Chelsea House. 2004.

Tributsch, Helmut. "On The Reddish, Glittery Mud the Inca Used for Perfecting Their Stone Masonry." SDRP Journal of Earth Sciences & Environmental Studies 3 (1), 309-323. 2018.

Vecchio, Rick. "Discovery: the Inca Rebellion of 1536." https://www.fertur-travel.com/blog/2009/discovery-the-inca-rebellion-of-1536/.

Wilford, John Noble. "New World's first gunshot victim is uncovered in Peru." New York Times, June 19, 2007.

Wright, Kenneth R, with McEwan, Gordon & Wright, Ruth M. *Tipon: Water Engineering Masterpiece of the Incan Empire.* American Society of Civil Engineers, Reston, VA, 2006.

Ingram Content Group UK Ltd.
Milton Keynes UK
UKHW020359210623
423783UK00006B/70